D0779683

Praise for *Pedal Power*:

'A wonderful collection of cycling tales'
Mike Carter, author of *One Man and His Bike*

'There are plenty of books about bicycles, so it's refreshing that *Pedal Power* is about people, not machines — it's full to the brim with inspiring pen portraits of the men and women who have helped to shape cycling and continue to shape it today.'
Carlton Reid, executive editor, BikeBiz.com, author of *Roads Were Not Built for Cars*

'A snappy exploration of all things bicycle that will inspire and motivate you'
Alastair Humphreys, author of *Microadventures*

'This belongs on the shelves of everyone who owns a bicycle.'
Dave Cornthwaite, author of *Life in the Slow Lane*

PEDAL POWER

Copyright © Anna Hughes, 2017

All rights reserved.

No part of this book may be reproduced by any means, nor transmitted, nor translated into a machine language, without the written permission of the publishers.

Anna Hughes has asserted her right to be identified as the author of this work in accordance with sections 77 and 78 of the Copyright, Designs and Patents Act 1988.

Condition of Sale
This book is sold subject to the condition that it shall not, by way of trade or otherwise, be lent, resold, hired out or otherwise circulated in any form of binding or cover other than that in which it is published and without a similar condition including this condition being imposed on the subsequent purchaser.

Summersdale Publishers Ltd
46 West Street
Chichester
West Sussex
PO19 1RP
UK

www.summersdale.com

Printed and bound by CPI Group (UK) Ltd, Croydon, CR0 4YY

ISBN: 978-1-78685-006-5

Photograph on page 4: James Carnegie Photography

Substantial discounts on bulk quantities of Summersdale books are available to corporations, professional associations and other organisations. For details contact general enquiries: telephone: +44 (0) 1243 771107, fax: +44 (0) 1243 786300 or email: enquiries@summersdale.com.

Disclaimer: although every effort has been made to ensure the details of the accounts presented herewith are entirely accurate, we apologise in advance for any unintentional omission, neglect or inaccuracy and will be pleased to amend any details and acknowledge companies or individuals in any subsequent edition of this publication.

ANNA HUGHES

PEDAL
POWER

INSPIRATIONAL STORIES FROM
THE WORLD OF CYCLING

summersdale

About the Author

Anna Hughes is a freelance writer, cycling instructor and mechanic. A passionate cycling tourist and traveller, her various adventures have taken her around the coast of the UK by bike and by boat, along the spine of Britain from Land's End to John o'Groats, and through the rigours of an Ironman. She lives on a narrowboat on the River Lea in east London.

CONTENTS

*The bicycle, the bicycle surely,
should always be the vehicle
of novelists and poets.*
CHRISTOPHER MORLEY

INTRODUCTION

I recently taught a ten-year-old girl how to ride a bicycle. Older than most of the children I teach, she had passed that stage of innocent abandon, when the stabilisers come off and just a push and some encouragement will do. The feeling of pressure was growing; she felt embarrassed to admit to her friends that she wouldn't go to the park with them because she couldn't ride a bike. It was such a simple yet significant thing. In our lesson she was determined and focussed, persevering even though it was hard work and the saddle was uncomfortable and she kept losing her balance. Her smile when she pedalled independently for the first time was incredible. She made me a card saying, 'Thank you for teaching me to ride a bike. It was the best day of my life. I will never forget it.'

Most people remember when they learned to ride a bike; I can vaguely recall my own first tentative attempt, wobbling down next door's drive. Riding a bicycle means freedom. And it's that freedom that can take us anywhere: to the park with friends, to school, to university or work, to the shops, to the countryside, on holiday. It can take us further afield, following in the footsteps of adventurers such as Dervla Murphy and Alastair Humphreys. It can lead to the world of sport – where speed, strength and skill are nurtured – through road racing, track racing or BMX, finding inspiration in such masters as Eddy Merckx and Laura Trott. It can be used as a way back to health from injury, a respite from mental health problems, or as an adrenaline rush for those who seek the thrill of downhill mountain biking, difficult terrain or extreme height.

The bicycle has huge historical importance, from the women who used it as a symbol of independence in their fight for liberation, to the workers who had a means of escaping to the countryside for the weekend, and the 'Good Roads' campaigners who literally paved the way for the road networks of today.

For me, the bicycle has always been important. It was a passport to exploration when I was a child, an independent means of getting to school as I got a bit older and a cheap way of travelling when I was a cash-strapped student. As an adult, it was a way of keeping fit on the way to work and it eventually became my work when I began teaching cycling for a living. It has also been my gateway to adventure: in 2011 I cycled 4,000 miles around the coast of the UK, leading to my book *Eat, Sleep, Cycle: A Bike Ride Around the Coast of Britain*, which details the adventures to be had on two wheels. Through cycling I have met many people and made many friends. I have been on protest rides and leisure rides, I have joined groups who use the bicycle as a tool for social change, and I have raised awareness as well as money.

This book is a collection of stories, from every aspect of cycling, that have inspired me and many others throughout the ages, and which will continue to inspire people for a long time to come. I hope you too will be inspired.

CHAPTER ONE

BEGINNINGS

James Moore – Winner of the world's first race

*I will get there first, or they
will find my body in the road.*

The 1850s saw the emergence of the rudimentary bicycle, a body-jarring, solid wooden contraption with strips of metal as tyres, which shook its rider to the core as it rattled down the uneven streets of the day. Aptly named the 'bone-shaker', this was an evolution of the striding machine that had been invented in 1817: a two-wheeled velocipede ('fast foot') propelled forwards by the rider's feet on the ground, which had become popular among the 'dandies' who could afford such luxuries. Towards the second half of the century, pedals were added to the front wheel, and in the late 1850s the French company Michaux began mass-producing these new velocipedes in Paris.

James Moore, an Englishman, lived opposite the Michaux family and became friendly with them; he spent many hours riding around Paris on his velocipede and running errands for his father from the city to the suburbs.

Popular among young gentlemen, the velocipede soon became more than just a vehicle: riders took to showing off on their machines to impress ladies or to beat friends and rivals, and groups of them would pedal through the city's parks, trying to outdo each other. In 1868 the Olivier brothers, partners in Michaux et Cie, decided to capitalise on this rivalry and staged a race at the Parc de Saint-Cloud in Paris. Five riders took part, including James Moore, who won. Such was the event's popularity that more races followed; the Englishman's prowess grew as he continued to participate, earning him the nickname The Flying Parisian.

In 1869 the Olivier brothers and the magazine *Le Vélocipède Illustré* organised what was to be the world's first road race: Paris to Rouen, 123 km through the valley of the Seine, to be completed in 24 hours. 'Bicycles should not be pulled by dogs or use sails,' stated the rules, and the winner would get 1,000 gold Francs and a bicycle. Moore lost no time in signing up – 'I will get there first, or they will find my body in the road,' he declared.

As more than 300 riders lined up at the start, chaos seemed certain to ensue; in a panic, the organisers split the group into two waves, evens and odds, to start 30 minutes apart. Moore drew number 187. He would be in the second wave.

His starting bell sounded and Moore gave chase into the rain of that damp day, soon leaving the other competitors behind. After just 12 miles he caught up with the stragglers of the first group who were pushing their machines up the hill into Saint-Germain-en-Laye. Moore pedalled hard up the incline, though later he would also have to get off and push – gears had yet to be invented. Slowly and steadily, he caught up to and overtook each of the other riders, many of whom had abandoned the race. In all, 32 riders finished in the time allowed, and James Moore was the fastest of them all, winning the race in 10 hours and 25 minutes – 15 minutes ahead of his nearest competitor. So fast was his ride that the mayor of Rouen, who was to present the trophies, had only just stepped off his carriage as Moore crossed the finishing line.

It was power, courage and determination that helped James Moore become the winner of the world's first road race – and a little invention called the ball bearing. His was the only bicycle in the race to use this addition to the front wheel, allowing smooth rotation and a more efficient use of pedalling energy.

The race was so successful that it inspired others across Europe: that same year the first London to Brighton race was held, in 1891 came Bordeaux–Paris – a 560 km ride ending at L'Arc de Triomphe – and then the Paris–Brest–Paris, an exhausting non-stop 1,260 km ride. In 1896 the first of what are now familiarly known as the Monuments was staged: Paris–Roubaix, a famously brutal ride on rough terrain and cobblestones, which is still raced today.

Thomas Stevens – Around the world on a penny-farthing

Stevens shan't have all the glory,
Though you are but pulseless steel;
Your part, too, shall live in story:
This was Thomas Stevens' wheel.
FROM 'AN ODE TO THOMAS STEVENS' (ANONYMOUS)

It was in the 1870s that the 'high wheeler' arrived – the next fad in the bicycle craze. Velocipedes had fixed axles: one pedal rotation equalled one wheel rotation, thus limiting the speed of the bicycle according to the size of the wheel. The solution: to build a larger wheel. Front wheels reached sizes of over 60 inches in diameter, complemented by a small wheel at the back, relative in size to the penny and the farthing. A nickname was coined.

High wheelers were popular among athletic well-to-do gentlemen, and racing and touring became a common pastime. In 1871 the racer James Moore bought one: the Ariel, patented by James Starley, a self-taught engineer and sewing machine manufacturer from London.

Riding schools were set up to teach folk how to master the wheel. The writer Mark Twain learned in the 1880s, penning a hilarious account of the experience in his essay 'Taming the Bicycle'. After causing his instructor to be hospitalised by repeatedly landing on top of him, he eventually perfected the 'voluntary dismount' – only after having perfected the involuntary one. Nevertheless, he loved riding and wrote in conclusion: 'Get a bicycle. You will not regret it, if you live.'

Thomas Stevens, a free spirit and explorative soul, lived in San Francisco, where he would listen to the constant whispering of the Pacific Ocean and dream of adventure – and what better adventure than to ride across the United States of America, in search of the opposite coast? In 1884 he set out on his Columbus penny-farthing, whose large front wheel measured 50 inches and heavy frame weighed 34 kg. He carried a change of socks, a spare shirt and a raincoat inside bags lashed beneath his seat, as well as a revolver strapped to his hip. For shelter he planned to sleep beneath his raincoat or rely on strangers' hospitality. Eastwards he rode, following in the wheels of several others who had attempted the journey, though all had failed and turned back. There followed several months of riding, dragging and pushing his bike along wagon roads, railroads, canal towpaths and the few public roads that existed. Poor weather and rough terrain meant that around a third of his journey was spent walking.

The perils of the journey were many: at one point he escaped a mountain lion by using his revolver; another time he was bitten by a rattlesnake, though the poisonous fangs sank harmlessly into his canvas gaiters. But more dangerous than wild animals was the railroad; though ideal in many ways – a route flat and direct, its network of tunnels and bridges carving a smooth passage through state after state – the rumble of an approaching train would cause Stevens's heart to beat fast in his chest. Once, he was forced to crouch beneath the tracks to avoid being hit, high above a ravine, his bicycle dangling in one hand.

Once he reached Boston, Stevens had achieved his aim: here was the Atlantic, to whose great waves he could now deliver the message of the Pacific. He spent the winter in New York, writing up the accounts of his travels for *Outing* magazine. Inspired by his work, the editors offered him sponsorship for his onward journey, if he chose to take it. So in April 1885 Stevens set sail for England for the next stage of what had become a round-the-world mission.

Through England, Europe and the Balkans he pedalled, then across Turkey, Iraq and Iran. In every nation he drew fascinated stares, folk intrigued by this tall, energetic white man with a curled moustache, riding a contraption which had never been seen before. Curious locals frequently blocked his path, asking him to entertain them with his bicycle. Though happy to oblige, this eventually became tiresome: when resting and eating at a cafe in Turkey the proprietor took away Stevens's unfinished meal, not returning it until he had pleased the crowds. Yet Stevens's overwhelming impression was of helpful, kind and hospitable people, willing to provide shelter, food and water. 'Humanity is the same the world over,' he wrote in his diary – a theme that would become familiar in the tales of generations of world travellers to come.

Refused passage by the authorities in Afghanistan, he retraced his steps back to the Mediterranean, where he took a ship to Karachi and rode the Grand Trunk Road to Calcutta. 'India is hotter than I could imagine,' he wrote, though it was one of the most fascinating places he had ever come across. Another boat took him to Hong Kong from where he travelled through eastern China, a place he described as chaotic, with rioters taking to the streets. Caught up in the madness, he sought shelter with Chinese officials. After this, Japan felt like a haven. From there he took a steamer back to San Francisco, 32 months after he had departed, with 13,500 miles under his wheels.

It was a key age for development and progress – a time of endless invention, though many feared technology as unnatural and devilish. But Stevens's travels demonstrated that the bicycle was not an invention to mar nature, but rather a tool through which folk could appreciate it all the more. Indeed, he was travelling neither as a soldier nor a preacher, but simply to satisfy a curiosity about people and the world.

An article in *The New York Times* written during his travels said:

> *But how the world shrinks and what a prospect does the adventurous cyclist open up before the eyes of wheelmen! What corner of the world will be left unvisited by the silent riders of the iron steed?... The inventor of the bicycle has done more to revolutionize the religious, moral and social ideas of mankind than all the philosophers of our time.*

John Kemp Starley – Roving on the Rover safety bicycle

My aim was not only to make a safety bicycle, but to produce a machine which should be the true Evolution of the Cycle.

Being the nephew of the great inventor James Starley, it was no surprise that John Kemp Starley would follow suit. As a protégé of his uncle, they would toil together in his workshop, and it was this legacy that would earn J. K. Starley a name as the inventor of the modern bicycle.

His uncle had developed the Ariel high wheeler: with a wire cross-spoked wheel, a hollow metal frame and rubber tyres, the ride offered significantly more comfort than its predecessor, the unyielding and heavy velocipede. However, the high wheeler had major safety considerations: direct drive made manoeuvrability difficult, fixed cranks meant that freewheeling was impossible and, with the rider mounted on the large front wheel, the centre of gravity was high, thus making the bicycle unstable – a bump in the road was all it could take to hurl the rider head first to the ground. 'Headers' were common and sometimes fatal. Something had to be done.

In 1880 the roller chain was invented by Hans Renold. This was what J. K. Starley had been waiting for: with the addition of a chain, the pedals could be taken off the front wheel, leaving it free to steer, and its size would no longer govern the speed of the bicycle. Starley strove to create the perfect machine in terms of comfort and practicality. Though simple, his requirements were revolutionary:

> To place the rider at the proper distance from the ground... to place the seat in the right position in relation to the pedals... to place the handles in such a position in relation to the seat that the rider could exert the greatest force upon the pedals with the least amount of fatigue.

Similar inventions emerged at the time, but none was as good as Starley's. Both wheels were of equal size, the rider's centre of gravity was in the middle of the bike, and the wire tangent spokes and rubber tyres would mean a comfortable ride. There were to be no more 'headers': the contraption was named 'the safety'.

The launch of the new bicycle was dismissed at first, derided by the gentlemen wheelers who saw the riders of these ground-level contraptions as 'crawlers' and 'beetles'. So, in order to prove his bike's worth, in 1885

Starley staged a 100-mile race from Norman Cross near Peterborough, along the Great North Road and finishing at Twyford in Berkshire. 'Safeties' and 'ordinaries' – the new name given to the penny-farthing, perhaps in an attempt to slight the new invention – lined up side by side on the start line. The gun sounded. Almost all of the 'safety' riders beat the time record.

J. K. Starley & Co was launched in 1889; in 1896 it was renamed the Rover Cycle Company. Though now better known for automobile manufacture, at the time it was one of the leading mass-producers of bicycles in the world. With the addition of John Dunlop's pneumatic tyre and the diamond-shaped frame, the modern bicycle was taking shape. J. K. Starley's model, the particulars of which remain largely unchanged in the bikes we use today, was copied by the entire cycle trade. 'The 'Rover', it was billed in advertisements, 'for ladies and gentlemen... has set the fashion to the world.'

William Rees Jeffreys – Paving the way

The greatest authority on roads in the United Kingdom and one of the greatest in the whole world.
DAVID LLOYD GEORGE

The railway boom in the 1840s brought to an end the coaching era, and many roads, unused and unmaintained, fell into disrepair. With surfaces made from stone setts, wooden blocks or rubber, the most pressing problem was dust: in dry weather it would billow in great clouds as cart and bicycle wheels kicked through it, whereas in poor weather the roads would be covered in mud. Manure was a huge contributing factor to the dirt: in 1894 *The Times* estimated that in the next half-century every London street would have been buried 9 feet deep in horse manure.

At first, the call for better-surfaced and maintained roads came from the rich who cycled for leisure and were the main sufferers of stuttering wheels and dust-filled air. The Cyclists' Touring Club (CTC) created the Roads Improvement Association (RIA) in 1885 which inspired the League of American Wheelmen (LAW) to establish the Good Roads movement. As cycling grew in popularity and safety bicycles became more common, more dust-choked riders added their voices to the campaign.

William Rees Jeffreys was born in London in 1872 and was a keen cyclist, throughout his teens exploring much of Britain by bike. In 1900 he was elected to the board of the CTC and became their representative on the Council of the RIA the following year. Fascinated by roads and networks, he had gained unparalleled knowledge during his travels, along with a deep frustration at their state of disrepair. He made it his life's work to address the problem of Britain's 'despaired and neglected roads'.

His proposals to improve the situation included bringing all roads under the control of a central board for improvement, with a national road classification system. He also floated the idea of a motorway 50 years before the first was built, and he proposed a circular boulevard around London for both cyclists and motorists. In addition, he suggested separating motor from pedal traffic, with parallel roads for wheelmen, a system now demonstrated in the Netherlands. But mostly, he campaigned against dust.

Practices in continental Europe led the way. In the 1890s, American president Woodrow Wilson regularly toured Europe on a bicycle along its well-surfaced roads, his experience preluding the Federal Highway Act in 1916, which led to the paving of America. Tar, or variations thereof, had been used since Roman times to create a surface suitable for transport. In 1902, Rees Jeffreys witnessed an experiment in Switzerland for the spreading of tar on the road between Geneva and Lausanne, and in 1907 he launched a competition to make a machine capable of performing the same task on Britain's roads.

In a matter of years, roads were sealed, greatly improving the quality of travel, the roadside environment and health in general.

Rees Jeffreys wrote in 1949: 'It is not only difficult, it is impossible, for the present generation to appreciate what their parents and grandparents suffered from dust and mud. Not only were houses made distressingly uncomfortable by dust, but household work was increased greatly by the mud and dust which children brought into the house on boots and clothes. The dust caused many ailments and diseases of the eyes, nose and throat.'

Largely forgotten in the drawers of history, and now far better lauded for being an arch-motorist, William Rees Jeffreys was one cyclist whose legacy can be enjoyed by riders of all vehicles to the present day.

'Few reforms brought so much direct benefit to the people as a whole as that which in so few years made the British roads dustless.'

Frances Willard – Conquering new worlds

*Bicycles are just as good company as most
husbands, and when they get shabby or old
a woman can dispose of it and get a new one
without shocking the entire community.*

ANN STRONG, *MINNEAPOLIS TRIBUNE*, 1895

The advent of the safety bicycle meant that cycling boomed. Starley's invention had universal appeal: anyone could do it, not just the tall, athletic types who were fit and rich enough to ride a high wheeler. It was a comfortable, reliable and cheap method of transportation for the working and middle class alike. Men and women could travel under their own steam; exploration increased and the gene pool widened.

But the craze sweeping across the Western world was deplored by some. The Women's Rescue League of America issued a resolution that denounced 'cycling's great curse', warning that riding caused 'diseases particular to women' and encouraged the evil that was associated with sport. Cycling was seen as unladylike and unchristian; it was cited as causing both sexual satisfaction and infertility.

Frances Willard was one of the most well-known Americans of her time. A leading suffragist and founder of the Women's Christian Temperance Union, she campaigned against the consumption of alcohol and promoted the bicycle as 'a more natural thrill', even though she did not, at the time, know how to ride.

Frances had been a free spirit as a young girl. Raised on a farm, she had spent much of her time in the fields, helping her father and playing – she even made her own plough.

But at the age of 16, she was brought inside, dressed in long skirts, corsets and hair pins, and 'tamed'. For this was her lot, as this was what society expected of women. Physically restricted by their clothes and financially restricted by their reliance on men, their role in life was as angels of the hearth and managers of the home. Known as the fairer – and certainly weaker – sex, women were never considered to be capable of excelling at anything. It was deemed unfeminine to be learned.

Women were discouraged from undertaking physical activity; perceived as timid and frail, they should be protected from danger. Few women were active, despite the emerging recognition that exercise was fundamental to health.

For all her achievements in the world of women's rights, Frances felt restricted in her life. She never forgot the freedom she had felt as a child, the satisfaction of doing things for herself. So in her fifties, she determined to learn to ride a bicycle. The experience was so liberating, exciting and revolutionary that she wrote a book: *A Wheel Within a Wheel; How I Learned to Ride the Bicycle*.

The bicycle had given her freedom: freedom from relying on men for transportation, freedom from the shackles of a society that would smother and protect her, and freedom from the gender differences that ruled every other aspect of her life. When she rode a bike, she was autonomous, empowered and equal.

A new world of sensations had been discovered: the thrill of speed, the buzz of exercise, the clarity of mind. She wanted other women to experience this wider world, which she believed to be key in the fight for women's rights. Once the bicycle was learned and conquered, the New Woman

could conquer new worlds. Her natural love of adventure –
a love long hampered and impeded – had been rediscovered
because of the bicycle, an 'implement of power'. By riding
a bicycle, a woman would 'become mistress of herself',
transformed into a 'rational, useful being restored to health
and sanity'.

> *I began to feel that myself plus
> the bicycle equaled myself plus
> the world, upon whose spinning
> wheel we must all learn to ride, or fall into
> the sluiceways of oblivion and despair.
> That which made me succeed with the
> bicycle was precisely what had gained me
> a measure of success in life – it was the
> hardihood of spirit that led me to begin,
> the persistence of will that held me to my
> task, and the patience that was willing to
> begin again when the last stroke had failed.
> And so I found high moral uses in the
> bicycle and can commend it as a teacher
> without pulpit or creed. She who succeeds
> in gaining the mastery of the bicycle will
> gain the mastery of life.*

The famous suffragist Susan B. Anthony later declared, 'I
think bicycling has done more to emancipate women than
anything else in the world... I stand and rejoice every time
I see a woman ride by on a wheel... the picture of free,
untrammeled womanhood.'

Tessie Reynolds – A pioneer of rational dress

*Miss Reynolds... is but the forerunner of a
big movement – the stormy petrel heralding
the storm of revolt against the petticoat.*
G. Lacy Hillier, *Bicycling News*, 1893

In September 1893, a young woman from Brighton cycled 120 miles to London and back in a record time of eight hours and 30 minutes. Aged just 16, her speed was remarkable. But what caused more of a stir at the time was the fact that she wore trousers.

Women in the late nineteenth century were expected to be modest in character and appearance: to wear feminine and becoming outfits consisting of floor-length skirts, tight jackets, corsets and voluminous petticoats. But such clothing was restrictive. Tessie Reynolds and her sisters had all been active from an early age, encouraged by their father to take up cycling, boxing and fencing. He was the secretary of a local cycling club and member of the National Cycling Union (NCU); her mother ran a boarding house in Brighton that welcomed cyclists. It had never been in her nature to wear clothing that would restrict her in the activities that she loved.

The question of women's emancipation was gaining momentum, pioneered by a call for clothing reform; the Rational Dress Society, founded in London in 1881, demanded that women should be able to wear clothes appropriate to their activities. In America, a certain Amelia Bloomer had developed a practical outfit consisting of a skirt worn over a pair of loose-fitting trousers or pantaloons.

Leading suffragist and advocate of cycling Frances Willard said, 'If women ride they must… dress more rationally than they have been wont to do. If they do this many prejudices as to what they may be allowed to wear will melt away.' Women campaigners couldn't fail to notice the irony that men's outfits were steadily being adjusted to allow them to ride their bicycles more easily – coat tails, for example, were made shorter to prevent them from becoming caught in the wheels. No such compensations were made for women.

As one cyclist of the time put it, 'A specialist adaption of dress is absolutely necessary, for skirts, while they have not hindered women from climbing to the topmost branches of higher education, may prove fatal in down-hill coasting.'

Tessie's ride in a rational outfit of knee-length breeches, a shirt and a long coat caused national outrage. In a time when it was scandalous for a woman to reveal her ankles, *Cycling* magazine described her outfit as 'of a most unnecessary masculine nature and scantiness'. She was accused of cycling in her knickerbockers.

Though she was not the first woman to wear such clothing, Tessie's ride attracted a huge amount of attention and was reported as far away as America: she had been racing, something that was not seemly for a woman; she had travelled through a number of towns on her way into central London, thereby exposing her female form to a large number of people; she rode a man's bicycle; and she was cheered on by a group of male pacemakers, including her father, who had acted as timekeeper. The authorities were appalled, *Cycling* magazine denounced it as a 'lamentable' incident and the *Yorkshire Evening Post* reported:

> *A pair of legs working like cranks on a pair of pedals is ugly enough in a man; but in a woman, especially with abnormal hips, the sight is a caricature of the sweetest and best half of humanity.*

In all likelihood many of the people she passed would not even have noticed that she was a woman. Perhaps Tessie was delighted with the attention – it certainly didn't put her off wearing that outfit, which had many more outings as she rode her bicycle.

However, it was men, rather than women, who set records in those days; Tessie's time did not officially count. Athleticism was discouraged as being dangerous to women's health; overexertion was blamed for heart disease, pneumatic disorders, overdeveloped muscles, nervous disorders and infertility. Tessie was taken to be examined afterwards by a medical man. Unsurprisingly, he found her to have suffered no ill effects from her ride.

There was much discussion of Tessie's outfit on the ladies' page of *Bicycling News*. She described her pantaloons as 'very comfortable and convenient' and women wrote letters asking for the pattern. The female editor wrote:

> *I think Miss Reynolds' costume is undoubtedly the cycling costume of the future, and I feel sure feminine cycling will reach, with its general adoption, to heights which are at present impossible for it. I congratulate*

Miss Reynolds on her courage in being an apostle of the movement.

Leading cycling expert of the time George Lacy Hillier wrote: 'A well-known cycling legislator recently remarked that he would like to set some of Miss Reynolds's critics the task of riding from Brighton to London and back with a skirt on.'

Tessie's fame brought her many letters of admiration and even marriage proposals, and she went on to be an advocate for women's cycling, promoting bicycles and racing – always wearing rational dress.

Tessie didn't set out to be a pioneer of women's rights nor of cycle sport, but it's indisputable that her ride as a daring young teenager helped both.

Arthur Zimmerman – The Jersey Skeeter

He is the best rider at the moment and perhaps the best ever. Everyone who has seen him agrees that he deserves to be called the king of the track.

FRENCH NEWSPAPER *VÉLOCE-SPORT*, JUNE 1893

In 1890s America, the bicycling craze was at its height: one in every 30 people owned a bicycle, thousands of miles of dedicated 'wheelways' were constructed and cycling became the national sport of the USA.

Nearly every state and country fair held bicycle races as an attraction. Major cities boasted race tracks constructed from dirt, cement or smooth banked wooden boards. More than 600 professionals rode the circuit on these velodromes. There they would vie for prizes, reputation and the thrill of the chase in races covering distances ranging from a quarter of a mile to 25 miles. Soon afterwards came the gruelling six-day races, where riders would cycle non-stop for 142 hours or until exhaustion took them.

Arthur Augustus Zimmerman of New Jersey had an astounding reputation: nicknamed the Jersey Skeeter, he had allegedly won 47 races in one week and finished some seasons with more than 100 victories. He had exceptional acceleration and the ability to pedal uncommonly fast, preferring a low gear, as he believed that more force would result in less speed.

The first international body for racing was the International Cycling Association (ICA), an organisation established by Henry Sturmey, who would later become famous as one half of the Sturmey-Archer company. In 1893, they staged the first Cycling World Championships in Chicago. Competitors lined up from countries including Germany, South Africa and the USA to contest races across three distances: 1 mile, 10 km and 100 km with a motor-pacer. The winner of each race would win a gold medal, with silver going to all other participants. Zimmerman won both the 10 km race and the 1 mile sprint.

Those two gold medals were added to a haul that included, in the single year of 1893, 15 bicycles, 15 jewellery rings, 15 diamonds, 14 medals, two cups, eight watches, a tract of land, six clocks, four scarf pins, nine pieces of silverware, two wagons and a piano.

His exceptional speed attracted the eye of Raleigh, who used his image to promote their bicycles: perhaps the first advertising of its kind and an early example of celebrity. Zimmerman was proclaimed as the Raleigh Champion of the World, and soon after his World Championship triumph, he travelled to Europe to race in France as a professional. With his reputation preceding him, the French were expecting something of a superman and were slightly bemused by this modest character who walked around with his hands in his pockets and an air of indifference.

The French newspaper *Véloce–Sport* reported that:

> *On the track, he wears nothing but black. He wears socks, but lets them fall around his ankles. His shorts don't fit him well. His jersey is not only not fresh but seems to be dirty. It is said that it has never been washed and never will be... Zimmerman is perhaps afraid his luck will run out if it is washed.*

He was not a dandy, they said, but a modest, well-mannered, shy man, who would blush and stammer when required to give a speech. But his racing told a different story; once on the track, he would 'whip the world', his acceleration unmatched, his speed unbeatable and his style unusual:

> *When the pace picks up, all his body movement stops as it is an obstacle to speed. Our best riders tend to bend their arms, to arch their*

backs, to move their head and shoulders, but Zimmerman simply pedals faster... His legs rotate with absolute regularity like the pistons of a locomotive.

During the French leg of his 1895 tour, he obliterated the field to the point where the officials were concerned his obvious dominance would become tiresome. 'Arthur, could you show us something different – to please the crowd?' they asked. 'After the bell,' he muttered in reply, remaining calmly at the very back of the pack until the bell announced the final lap, when, in the sprint along the final straight, he stormed past the entire group at a stupefying speed to once more take the victory.

His fame and success led him to race all over the world. The strain of constant travelling and racing eventually caught up with him and he retired in 1905; in a career of little over a decade he had won over 1,000 races. He was the first world champion: an early celebrity and an inspiration for cyclists all over the world.

Annie Londonderry – Around the world in 450 days

I am a journalist and a 'new woman'.

It took a remarkable woman to set off to ride a bicycle around the world in 1890s America: Annie Kopchovsky had a husband, three children and responsibilities as a housewife. It was not just a novelty for a young woman to leave those duties, but to do it in pursuit of a world bicycle tour was unheard of. The wager that set her off on her adventure might have been a myth: in a time of emerging world travel and public fascination with round-the-world efforts, inspired perhaps by Phileas Fogg in the 1873 novel *Around the World in 80 Days*, two men had reportedly made the claim that no woman could encircle the globe on a bicycle within 15 months while also earning $5,000. Annie took up the bet.

Perhaps it was an honest bet; perhaps she fabricated it as her token to adventure, fame and freedom from her home life – either way, she set off from Boston, Massachusetts, in June 1894 on a 42-pound Columbia women's bicycle, with a change of clothes and a pearl-handled revolver. Incredibly, she had never ridden a bicycle before accepting the challenge; a couple of lessons were her only preparation. She was to seek out the American consuls in the cities she visited as proof of travel, and the required $5,000 earnings would come from carrying advertising boards. Her first sponsor was Londonderry Lithe Spring Water, whose payment of $100 had come on the condition that she adopt their brand as her name. This she duly did, and her alter ego was born: Mlle Londonderry, daring world-traveller.

Riding westwards she soon reached Chicago, where the whole venture nearly came to a premature end. Perhaps it was the exertion of riding as a novice, the heavy bicycle and even heavier skirts, or the looming mountains and plains, and the oncoming winter. It had taken several months to reach that point and the clock was ticking on her 15-month wager. *The New York Times* reported her decision to abandon the journey, and she turned back, ready to retrace her steps home. But before returning she exchanged her clunky bicycle for a man's 21-pound Sterling and adopted a man's riding suit. More suitably dressed, on a lighter bicycle and certainly physically fitter than when she had departed, she arrived back on the east coast once more dedicated to the task. She boarded a boat from New York to France to continue her adventure.

Bold, charismatic and beautiful, she captured the imagination of the world's press: stories of her billboard-laden bicycle appeared frequently in news reports. Labelled the 'intrepid traveller', she sought sponsorship wherever she went, making public appearances, selling pictures and giving outlandish interviews where she would spin wildly improbable accounts of her travels. She proved to be an excellent speaker, enthralling audiences with her tales, and an excellent rider, reportedly joining in cycling events and races in the places through which she passed. Posters and placards covered her and her bicycle, and she was often dressed head to toe in ribbons advertising anything from milk to perfume.

But it had been a slow start and Annie had lost much time. In order to be home within the 15 months, she needed to pick up the pace, so after riding south through France, she boarded a boat across the Mediterranean to the Middle East, cycling through Saudi Arabia and Yemen before another boat trip landed her in China. Short cycle trips in Korea and Japan were followed by a Pacific crossing by steamer. 'She has a degree of self-assurance somewhat unusual to her sex,' reported the *San Francisco Chronicle* as she arrived back in the United States.

From San Francisco to El Paso on the Texan border she pedalled, then journeyed up through the mid states to Chicago by bicycle and train, finally arriving back to Boston 450 days after her departure. Though more a journey with a bike than a journey on a bike, she won her wager, and proved herself a master of self-promotion and grit. It had not only been a simple test of a woman's physical and mental endurance, but a demonstration of how a woman could fend for herself in the world. On her return she moved her family to New York and wrote sensational articles for the *New York World* about her journey, calling herself the New Woman: 'If that term means I believe I can do anything that any man can do.' The *New York World* hailed the trip as 'the most extraordinary journey ever undertaken by a woman'.

Her fame soon passed and she died in relative obscurity in 1947; her round-the-world ride was not even mentioned in the death notice placed by her family. It wasn't until the beginning of the twenty-first century that her story came to light once more; after some sustained detective work, her great-grandnephew Peter Zheutlin painstakingly pieced together her tale: the legend of Annie Londonderry, the first woman to bicycle around the world.

Marshall 'Major' Taylor – A black man in a white world

There are positively no mental, physical or moral attainments too lofty for the Negro to accomplish if granted a fair and equal opportunity.

It took courage, honesty and determination for Marshall Taylor to overcome racial intolerance and compete in a sport he loved. To become a world champion is a feat in itself, but to do so in the face of racial opposition is doubly remarkable.

Taylor was born in 1878 in the US state of Indiana to a poor family. He spent much of his childhood with the family for whom his father worked, who steadily adopted him into their home in a wealthy neighbourhood. They included Taylor in their meals, they schooled him along with their son and, aged 12, they bought him a bike. Taylor's skill was obvious from the start; he would spend hours practising tricks and stunts. However, when the family moved away, Taylor returned to his life of poverty, earning money from his paper round or running errands for which he rode his bicycle barefoot – there was little money for shoes.

His substantial bicycle skills caught the eye of the local bike shop owner, who employed him to perform tricks outside the shop to attract trade. He had to wear a military uniform, which earned him the nickname of 'Major Taylor'.

The owner of the shop entered the 13-year-old Marshall into a race, thinking it would be good for publicity. 'I know you can't go the full distance, but just ride up the road a little way, it will please the crowd, and you can come back as soon as you get tired,' he told Marshall at the start line. The pistol sounded and Marshall was off, roaring up the road and feeling adrenaline surging through his veins as he discovered a strength he'd never before known. He won the race and promptly collapsed in a heap.

The event had been a tantalising glimpse of his capabilities: for the next five years he continued to race, winning local competitions, and attracting the attention of sponsors and beneficiaries. But discrimination marred his involvement in the sport: as a black man, he was not allowed to join his local bicycle club and often he'd be shunned by the white cyclists at the events in which he participated.

Banned from competing locally, at the age of 15 he moved to Worcester, Massachusetts, a more racially tolerant area and the centre of the US bicycle industry at the time. The move was encouraged by his friend and mentor Louis D. 'Berdi' Munger, who owned the Worcester Cycle Manufacturing Company in Massachusetts. In 1896, Munger sneaked him into a whites-only race in Indianapolis. The organisers disallowed him, refusing him a pacer for his individual time trial. But the other competitors came to his aid: they mounted the pacing tandem themselves, leading him out onto the track. The crowd roared, cheering him across the line as he knocked 6 seconds off the world record. He tried again in the 1/5-mile race and beat the record by two-fifths of a second. The crowd went wild. Even though Marshall was barred from the track for the stunt, he had unofficially set a world record; the spectators knew they had witnessed something phenomenal.

He began competing in the hugely popular six-day races, a superhuman feat of endurance that saw competitors riding round the clock, day and night, and during which drugs such as nitroglycerin and cocaine were commonly used as stimulants. Sleep deprivation and drug-induced hallucinations got to him at his first professional race in Madison Square Gardens, where he declared, 'I cannot go on with safety, for there is a man chasing me around the ring with a knife in his hand.'

By 1898 Marshall held seven world records, including the standing mile, for which he recorded a time of 1:41 – a record that stood for 28 years. It was in 1899 that he competed in the World Championships in Montreal and became the sprint champion, earning himself a place in the history books as the second ever black world champion in any sport.

Worldwide he was known as the Black Cyclone, with a large following in Europe, though he was less well-received on home soil. The League of American Wheelmen refused membership to black people and he was banned from racing in many states. His competitors would jostle him and box him in, and spectators would throw ice and nails at him. After a race in Alabama he was attacked on the finish line by a rider who hadn't taken kindly to being beaten by a black man. He was throttled to the ground; at the insistence of the crowd, the police fined the man. Again and again, he attempted to enter the National Sprint championships but was always refused. It wasn't until 1900, when he was already World Sprint Champion and seven-time world record holder, that he was finally permitted.

At the height of his career he was earning $30,000 a year – more than most other athletes of the day, black or white – but interest in cycling was beginning to wane with the arrival of the automobile and he retired in 1910, aged 32.

After a string of bad investments and the Wall Street crash, Marshall's fortune was lost. He spent six years writing his autobiography, *The Fastest Bicycle Rider in the World*, which he self-published and sold door-to-door on the streets of Chicago. When he died, his body lay unclaimed in the morgue and was buried in an unmarked grave.

Some 12 years later a group of former racing cyclists and club members, with money donated by bicycle manufacturer Frank Schwinn, had his remains exhumed and buried in a more prominent part of Mt Glenwood Cemetery in Illinois. His gravestone reads:

" *World champion bicycle racer who came up the hard way— Without hatred in his heart—An honest, courageous and God-fearing, clean-living gentlemanly athlete. A credit to his race who always gave out his best—Gone but not forgotten.*

CHAPTER TWO

GRAND TOUR MASTERS

Maurice Garin – Winner of the first Tour de France

*With the broad and powerful swing of the
hand which Zola in* The Earth *gave to his
ploughman,* L'Auto, *journal of ideas and action,
is going to fling across France today those
reckless and uncouth sowers of energy who are
the great professional riders of the world.*
HENRI DESGRANGE

Henri Desgrange was looking for a way to boost business.
His newspaper, *L'Auto*, was struggling. A keen cyclist and
velodrome owner, he had seen how rival broadsheet *Le
Vélo* had benefitted from its sponsorship of the Bordeaux–
Paris and Paris–Roubaix, both long, gruelling feats of the
type popular at the time. Desgrange decided to create the
ultimate test of endurance: an event similar to the gruesome

challenge of the six-day race, but on roads and taking place over several weeks around the perimeter of France. He advertised a five-stage race lasting 36 days. Only 15 people entered. Desgrange cut the length to 2,500 km over 19 days and offered substantial prizes. On 1 July 1903, 60 cyclists gathered for the start of the inaugural Tour de France. Among their number was Maurice Garin.

Garin was a popular racing cyclist, nicknamed *le petit ramoneur* (the little chimney sweep), which he was by trade, or *le fou* (the madman) because of the speed with which he pedalled around the town. Since his first 24-hour race in Paris in 1893, where he was one of only two people to cross the finish line, he had raced Paris–Roubaix three times, and won both Paris–Brest–Paris and Bordeaux–Paris. Of gruelling length, on unforgiving roads, through inclement weather and through the night, such races drew huge crowds; the riders, who would suffer fatigue, pain and discomfort to reach the end were elevated to the status of supermen. To take part in the toughest race ever conceived was irresistible to Garin. Desgrange had said his ideal Tour would be one in which 'only one rider survived the ordeal'.

On the afternoon of 1 July, the cyclists set off from the Café Reveil-Matin in a village just outside Paris. Riding through the night, the riders pitted their wits and their strength against each other. Times would be recorded for the completion of each stage; the rider with the lowest aggregate time at the end would be announced the winner. Garin won the first stage and the second. Such were the physical demands of the race that by the end of the fourth stage, only 24 riders remained. After three weeks of riding, Garin won the final two stages to cross the finish line more than 64 hours ahead of the man who would come in last. 'The 2,500 km that I've just ridden seem a long line, grey and monotonous, where nothing stood out from anything else,' he said. 'I suffered on the road; I was hungry, I was thirsty, I was sleepy, I suffered, I cried.'

The brutal test of strength that Desgrange had envisaged had proved a huge success. Sales of *L'Auto* soared. Desgrange announced entries for the following year's race.

Garin once more took up the mantle, and once again, he won. But the race was marred by reports of cheating; riders were suspected of clinging on to cars and Garin was accused of taking the train. Spectators would conspire to help their favourites and hold back rivals. After being beaten up by a mob, Garin declared, 'I'll win the Tour de France provided I'm not murdered before we get to Paris.' Crossing the finish line in first place, unable to prove his innocence from cheating, Garin was stripped of his title. He never won a race again.

And that was nearly that; Desgrange announced that the Tour would run no more. But by the following year he'd changed his mind, announcing shorter stages, with daytime-only racing to ensure that all entrants would abide by the rules. Apart from during the war years, the Tour de France has run every year since.

Desgrange's race set a precedent for the Giro d'Italia and Vuelta a España, the two other races that now make up the Grand Tours. The Giro was launched in 1909 to boost sales of *La Gazzetta dello Sport*, while the Vuelta was instigated in 1935 by Spanish magazine *Informaciones*. The races are governed by the Union Cycliste International (UCI – set up in 1900 to replace the ICA) and teams race, as they initially did, for a sponsor (though they briefly raced for national teams).

The Tour de France is still the most eminent of all the Grand Tours, and the coveted yellow jersey – the colour of *L'Auto*'s pages – introduced in 1919 to be worn by the race leader is a recognised symbol all over the world. Over time, the stages have become shorter and no longer run in a continuous loop. The race always follows a different route, consisting variously of mountain stages, flat stages and time trials, and since 1975 has always ended at the Champs-Élysées in Paris.

Fame and fortune still await those who can finish, and win, the most prestigious bicycle race in the world.

Fausto Coppi – Il Campionissimo

Once Coppi had broken away from the
peloton, the peloton never saw him again.
PIERRE CHANY, FRENCH CYCLING JOURNALIST

It was in the 1940s that a hero emerged: the kind of rider who could not only win a Grand Tour, but could do so again and again – and go on winning. Fausto Coppi became known as 'Il Campionissimo', the 'Champion of Champions', the first rider to dominate the Giro d'Italia, winning it five times. An excellent all-rounder, superior at climbing as well as time trialling and sprinting, his formidable form lasted throughout the 1940s and 1950s.

His strong features and solid riding became a familiar sight as he steamrolled up a mountain while the pack scattered below him, one by one dropping away. Racing was different then: with no helmet or sunglasses, he would ride with a spare tyre slung over his shoulders.

The one-day classics were by then firmly established in the international racing calendar, the five Monuments the most prestigious of these: Milan–San Remo, the Tour of Flanders, Paris–Roubaix, Liège–Bastogne–Liège and Giro di Lombardia.

Coppi came to the notice of the world when, aged 20, he was drafted into the team for the 1940 Giro d'Italia to support Gino Bartali, team leader and winner of the 1938 Tour de France. To everyone's astonishment, Coppi won, becoming the Giro's youngest ever winner. Bartali was indignant. There followed a decade-long battle between the two countrymen, which split the nation into Coppiani and Bartaliani: while Bartali was religious, traditionalist and conservative, Coppi was innovative, cosmopolitan and secular. The former was a devoted husband, whereas the latter was known for his marital indiscretions. Bartali was teetotal; Coppi regularly took *la bomba*: a mixture of cola, caffeine and amphetamines (while frowned upon, doping was not prohibited at that time). The pair fought against each other to win the race and the hearts of Italy.

More often than not, Coppi came out on top. In the one-day classics he notched up victory after victory. In the 1946 Milan–San Remo, Coppi and nine other riders launched the attack just 5 km into the 292 km race. On the first mountain pass, less than halfway through the race, he steadily dropped every one of the nine riders, powering upwards at a rate impossible to match. He won the race 14 minutes ahead of the second-place rider – and more than 18 minutes ahead of Bartali.

In the 1948 World Championships, they locked horns, neither wishing to help the other, riding slower and slower and eventually bowing out of the race. The Italian cycling association denounced their performance, saying: 'Thinking only of their personal rivalry, they abandoned the race, to the opprobrium of all sportsmen.' Both riders were suspended for three months. The rivalry nearly put them both out of the Tour the following year, the pair bickering as the peloton slipped further ahead. Under pressure from their team, they made peace and, with a deficit of 55 minutes, Coppi put on a magnificent display through the Alps, clawing back the lead to win overall. It was his first Tour win, to add to his Giro win that spring: the first time any cyclist had won both in the same year.

In 1952, the Alpe d'Huez – now a regular feature in the Tour – was included for the first time. Coppi won the climb, and the Tour, by over 28 minutes. The organiser had to double the prizes for the lower placings in order to keep the other riders interested. His win, making a Giro/Tour double again, cemented his place in history.

After the 1953 World Championships, news of an affair came out: Coppi had been indiscreet with the wife of an army captain and adultery was at that time a criminal offence in Italy. The scandal meant that in the 1954 Giro d'Italia, Pope Pius XII, who would traditionally receive riders and bless the *maglia rosa* (the winner's pink jersey), refused to do so. Spectators turned their backs on Coppi; some even spat at him. He was put on trial for adultery in 1955 and received a suspended sentence. Coppi ended up marrying his mistress and having a child with her, though neither was recognised by the Italian State.

He died just five years later from a virus contracted while in Africa. It was a tragic conclusion to what had been a somewhat troubled life, but in tribute to his supreme performance as a rider and climber, organisers of the Giro added a mountain bonus: the *Cima Coppi*, awarded to the rider who reaches the Giro's highest summit ahead of the rest of the field, as Coppi did countless times in his extraordinary career.

Jacques Anquetil – Monsieur Chrono

To prepare for a race, there is nothing better than a good pheasant, some champagne and a woman.

Many sports stars' stories are best told through their rivalries, and Jacques Anquetil is no exception. The first cyclist in history to win the Tour de France five times, and the dominant force on road and track in the 1960s, he remained frustrated throughout his career that, though he won races, he never won the hearts of the French people. That accolade was awarded to Raymond Poulidor, Anquetil's countryman and rival who, despite riding 14 Tours in his long career, never once wore the *maillot jaune*. The French loved the humble underdog, the eternal second, preferring him to Anquetil's cold and calculating demolition of the field.

Anquetil's performance in time trialling was unmatched, earning him the title Monsieur Chrono. He would out-sprint the rest of the field, clocking up huge wins in the time trial stages, and then do just enough in the mountains to cling on to the yellow jersey. He won the Tour de France on his debut in 1957 and famously said before his next attempt in 1961 that he would 'take the yellow jersey on day one and wear it till the end'. That's exactly what he did. He went on to win every year for the next four years. He was the first cyclist to win all three of the Grand Tours, taking the *maglia rosa* in the Giro d'Italia in 1960 and 1964, and the *jersey roja* in the Vuelta a España in 1963.

Serious, blond and with film-star looks, Anquetil's style of riding had elegance and fluidity; he appeared to cruise while others wriggled. Perhaps this is why the French public never warmed to him; he made it look too easy, as if he weren't really suffering. Even on the ascent of the Puy de Dôme in the 1964 Tour de France, where a fabulous duel played out between Aloof Anquetil and Passionate Poulidor, he failed to win them over. The superior climber, Poulidor should easily have won the stage. But Anquetil stuck with him for an incredible 10 km, battling it out in an elbow-clashing fight, riders shoulder to shoulder, swaying towards and away from each other, with legs and bikes almost touching. Together they ascended, side by side up the narrow mountain road, neither giving an inch, by sheer force of will matching each other pedal for pedal. Eventually, Poulidor dropped his challenger, though his stage victory wasn't enough to win him the Tour: it was Anquetil who went on to attain his record-setting fifth Tour win. Therein lay Anquetil's greatest frustration: despite his historic achievement, despite putting his name in the record books for the French, it was Poulidor they hailed as the hero for winning that climb.

The duelling would bring to an end his Tour career. He couldn't face riding it the following year and withdrew the year after that owing to bad health.

Raphaël Géminiani, a former racer and Anquetil's manager, gave this insight into Anquetil's character:

> *People said he was cold, a calculator, a dilettante. The truth is that Jacques was a monster of courage. In the mountains, he suffered as though he was damned. He wasn't a climber, but with bluffing, with guts, he tore them to shreds.*

He was treated badly by the crowds, who whistled and hissed at him, and by the organisers, who shortened the time trial stages so he would lose.

Géminiani again:

> *More than once, I saw him crying in his hotel room after suffering the spitting and insults of spectators.*

Anquetil was always open about his use of drugs, which were necessary, he said, like 'a geography teacher taking aspirin for a headache'. Up until the 1950s, races were reported with heroism, the riders viewed as gods and sufferers, and the use of drugs was overlooked. But in the 1960s attitudes began to change, and following the death in 1967 of British rider Tom Simpson, who had collapsed on the ascent of Mont Ventoux with amphetamines in his blood, public opinion turned. Anquetil's view was no longer accepted. The French team quietly dropped him and he pointedly raced his last race outside France, in Antwerp.

Eddy Merckx – The Cannibal

*Ride as much or as little, or as long or
as short as you feel. But ride.*

They called him the Cannibal, a phenomenon who dominated the sport in the late 1960s and 1970s, devouring the field in almost every race he entered. Merckx has since come to be known as the greatest rider ever to have taken to the world stage. Over a 13-year career, he won 525 races, including more Tour de France stages and Grand Tour stages than any other rider in history. The Belgian was the first to achieve the Triple Crown of cycling: victory in the Tour, Giro d'Italia and World Championships in one season. His number of Grand Tour wins, totalling 11, has yet to be beaten.

In the 1969 Tour de France he not only won overall, but also took the points classification and the mountains classification – the only cyclist ever to have done so. In 1968 he had done the same in the Giro. His performance in the Monuments was unmatched: he won each of them at least twice, including the Liège–Bastogne–Liège a record five times and the Milan–San Remo a record seven times.

A bronze and stone monument listing his achievements stands on the Côte de Stockeu, one of the climbs in the Liège–Bastogne–Liège, as a tribute to the great man. It simply ends with the word 'etc.'.

With an insatiable appetite for winning, very few people got a look-in when Merckx was in the field. The image of him holding his arms or his victor's flowers aloft was one which came to dominate the sport. *Cycling* magazine said: 'Eddy Merckx, the complete champion, has the Tour de France in his pocket.' His dominance of the Tour led the French press to declare, 'Gentlemen, this is a catastrophe!' running headlines such as: 'Merckx – Is he going to kill the Tour de France?'

But races in which he was involved were hard-fought and dramatic – it wasn't just that he won; it was how he won. He was known for attacking relentlessly, riding with the breakaway group and then launching an attack, often early and on his own. At the 1969 Tour of Flanders, he headed away from the breakaway with 45 miles to go. Ignoring his team's insistence that he stop, he carried on, alone, through wind and rain, to win. On the seventeenth stage of the 1969 Tour de France, with over 8 cumulative minutes on his nearest rival, he attacked alone on the last two mountain climbs, winning that stage by another 8 minutes. With astounding brilliance, this unbelievable show of strength and ability led to victory after victory, his greed for the win giving him a capacity to push through the pain: 'The race is won by the rider who can suffer the most.'

However, the crowd never went wild for Merckx; he was admired rather than loved, respected rather than adored. His nicknames were brutish: the Cannibal, and in Italy *il mostro* – the monster. Perhaps it was the predictability of the win: when Merckx was on the start line, the rest of the field knew their battle would be for second place. When told that he won too much, he would say, 'The day I start a race without intending to win it, I won't be able to look at myself in the mirror.' Despite his incredible record, he would remain anxious at the start line that this would be the race that he wouldn't win, that whatever he had to give wouldn't be enough. Perhaps that's why he pushed so hard – just in case, for in cycle racing, the win is never guaranteed. 'Every year you start anew, and you have to get your diploma again.'

A crash on the track in 1969 nearly ended his career. Riding behind a derny – a mechanised pacer bike – another cyclist crashed, taking Merckx and his pacer out with him. The derny rider was killed instantly and Merckx, who was knocked unconscious, cracked his vertebrae and twisted his pelvis. He spent the rest of his career riding through the pain.

In 1975 Merckx was on course for an unprecedented sixth Tour de France victory, his rival for the podium the Frenchman Bernard Thévenet. As is traditional in the Tour, spectators line the road with no barriers to hold them back. They close in on the riders and can ultimately influence the result – a stray bag strap is all that is needed to bring a rider down. Perhaps it was the French rallying around their man, but during the climb up Puy de Dôme, a spectator lunged forwards and punched Merckx hard in the stomach. It was a rare breach of the spectator/rider agreement, a shocking incident that ultimately cost Merckx the victory. He would never win the Tour again.

The Milan–San Remo had been his very first victory in 1966, and the 1977 race would be his last. His form dropped; he'd been unable to win the Tour in the previous two years, and in 1978 he announced his retirement.

Only one major title had eluded him: Paris–Tours. After his own victory in 1972, the Belgian rider Noël Vantyghem said 'Between us, me and Eddy Merckx have won everything that can be won. I won Paris–Tours, he won all the rest.'

For that was his dominance: a rider who gobbled up the victories and never seemed to slake his thirst. The greatest rider of his generation, and of all time. Etc.

Bernard Hinault – The Badger

I race to win, not to please people.

Once the Merckx era was over, fans began searching around for someone to replace him: the next superhero who would face adversity and win for them at whatever cost. Along came Bernard Hinault, who in the 1980s equalled Merckx's Tour de France record and nearly matched his Grand Tour wins, with ten in total. He remains the last French winner of the Tour de France.

A tough character, he was strong-willed and outspoken, and often controversial. In his Tour debut in 1978, the split-stage format meant that riders had hardly any rest between one stage and the next. After only a handful of hours' sleep, Hinault led his fellow competitors in a protest, deliberately riding the stage slowly, arriving well after the finish time, before dismounting and walking across the line. Officials were forced to cancel the stage. A natural leader, he would often control the peloton – 'There will be no attacks today as tomorrow's stage will be difficult' – holding back and reducing the pace in dangerous conditions, sometimes allowing lesser teams to take a stage as long as it didn't affect the overall standings.

Common at the time was for groups of protestors to take to the roads during bicycle races, appropriating the media coverage for their own cause. When workers from a shipyard blocked the road during the 1984 Paris–Nice race, Hinault ploughed straight into them, instigating a now legendary punch-up.

'Merckx was the greatest but Hinault was the most impressive. I've never seen inner anger like his,' said 1976 Tour winner, Belgian Lucien van Impe. He didn't have to win all the time. 'But when he did want to win… he usually did so in emphatic style,' says Richard Moore, author of *Slaying the Badger*. One of the most consistent riders on the world stage, in the years he didn't win the Tour, he came second. But he could be arrogant and wouldn't pander to the public. An interviewer once remarked that he should pay more attention to the fans. He responded, 'I race to win, not to please people.'

The tougher the going, the more he seemed to enjoy himself. He had ridden the 1980 Liège–Bastogne–Liège on a course covered in snow, riding solo for the last 50 miles through a blizzard and, despite suffering frostbite, winning by 10 minutes. Of the starting line-up of 174, only 21 riders crossed the finish line. He went on to win the World Championships that year on one of the most difficult courses ever ridden, where hardly any riders finished. His spectacular win in the 1985 Tour was achieved despite a crash in the later stages which saw him ride the final week with two black eyes and a broken nose. This was the year of his record-equalling fifth title.

The 1986 Tour was his last outing, and he finished one stage alongside teammate and oft-time rival American Greg

LeMond, enabling the latter to retain the yellow jersey. Perhaps it was a gesture of gratitude, as LeMond had helped Hinault win the previous year. After that he retired, at the tender age of 32, quitting while he was ahead.

Miguel Induráin – Big Mig

You need brains to stay in the front.

At 6'2", Miguel Induráin didn't look like a champion of cycling. He lacked the litheness that other riders used to gallop up a mountain and the aerodynamism that helped them to speed to the finish line – yet, somehow, he still won. 'Amid the flat backs and skiers' crouches, Induráin rode like a Spanish galleon,' said Chris Sidwells in *A Race for Madmen*. But his advantage in the end was his size: 'His engine was so big that aerodynamic subtlety didn't matter so much.'

The Spaniard arrived on the Tour scene quietly, which was how he tended to do things: in a reserved and calm way, without making a fuss. 'When he comes down for his meal, you don't even hear him move his chair,' said ex-teammate Jean-Francois Bernard. In contrast to his predecessors, his Tour debut did not result in a win. He didn't even finish it – or his second. On his third try he came 97th, then 47th, then 17th, then 10th: a slow build-up to the podium which, once he reached it in 1991, he wouldn't relinquish for five years, equalling the record of the best Tour performances by the greats before him.

Big guys don't usually excel, especially in the mountains, but his physical capabilities were incredible: rumoured to have a resting heart rate of 28 bpm (the typical for athletes is 40 bpm), his cardiac output (volume of blood pumped by the heart) was 50 litres per minute and his VO2 max (maximum oxygen uptake) was 88 ml/kg/min – both double the human norm. According to his coach, his long thigh bones pumping away like pistons were his secret weapon. His speed in the time trials was devastating, and with runs of 150–200 km (as opposed to the 50–80 km that's more common today), he was at an advantage, steadily matching his rivals in the mountains and then calmly extending his lead in the time trial stages. It was the mentality of time trialling that he preferred: being out there on your own with no team to help or hinder – just you, the clock and the kilometres.

Criticised for not attacking more, for not leading a race, for riding defensively, he replied, 'The way I rode is the way I am.' He was hardly dazzling, but he was ruthlessly efficient. The elegance of his performances inspired future stars such as Bradley Wiggins and drew admiration from his teammates. It was his consistency and composure that led to so many victories: 'You need brains to stay in the front.'

Lance Armstrong – The fallen angel
(Armstrong is included as a significant figure at the time, despite the truth that finally emerged.)

I'm not going to be sorry for certain things. I'm going to be sorry for that person who was a believer, who was a fan, who supported me, who defended me, and ended up looking like a fool.

The revelations in 2012 that Lance Armstrong had consistently doped throughout his career brought an end to the reign of one of the most revered and successful cyclists on the planet. Armstrong won the Tour de France an unprecedented seven times. After an Anti-Doping Agency investigation named him as ringleader of 'the most sophisticated, professionalized and successful doping program that sport has ever seen', he was stripped of his titles and given a lifetime ban.

In a candid interview with Oprah Winfrey, Armstrong said that it would not have been humanly possible to win the Tour so many times without doping, and in doing so burst open a culture that had long been simmering beneath the surface, from Fausto Coppi's *la bomba* to Tom Simpson's amphetamines. A blank space occupies the table where Armstrong's Tour victories were listed, the doping suspected to be so rife that no riders were given honours in those years.

Seen by some as a scapegoat for a culture that drove riders to succeed at all costs and derided by others as a cheating scumbag, Armstrong splits opinion. Perhaps if he had not so emphatically denied doping throughout his winning years, he would now be more positively regarded.

Because his victories couldn't have been won on drugs alone. Armstrong was an incredible athlete, from his becoming a professional triathlete at the age of 15, to winning the 1993 World Road Race Championship at the record age of 21, to his first stage win in the 1995 Tour – a stage that he rode in tribute to teammate Fabio Casartelli, who had died after a fall on a mountain descent three days earlier.

Perhaps most remarkable of all, he survived the cancer that should have killed him, and fought an immense physical and mental battle after remission to return to front line competition.

Cyclists are accustomed to pain; they train themselves to push through it and embrace the suffering, so it was easy for Armstrong to ignore a groin complaint. It wasn't until he coughed up blood and one testicle had swollen to three times its normal size that he visited his doctor, expecting to be given some antibiotics for a virus and to be sent on his way. The diagnosis was chilling: cancer. He was barely 25. The next day the testicle was removed and 12 tumours, some as big as golf balls, were found in his lungs. Cancer was also discovered in his abdomen and lesions were found in his brain. He was told by his urologist that his chances of survival were 20–50 per cent, 'mainly to give him hope'. But in truth, his chances of survival were almost zero.

Yet Armstrong pulled through, and after three rounds of chemotherapy was back on his bike, training again a year after being declared cancer-free. He set up the Lance Armstrong Foundation, now the Livestrong Foundation, to give support and hope to those living with the illness.

Since the doping revelations, Armstrong has been shunned by the cycling world. His bullying and elaborate deception will never be forgiven by many, but children still enter the cancer ward clutching his book, knowing that his survival has given them hope.

Chris Froome – The future hope

*Chris Froome is a very great champion... he's
a good time triallist, he's good at ascents,
he's overall. He's the best of the moment.*
EDDY MERCKX

Chris Froome is one of the strongest climbers of his time. Yet he rides under the cloud of Lance Armstrong's legacy. People spit at him, shout *'Dopé!'*, mimic injecting their arms as he rides past. The spectators get up close, one upturning a cup of urine over his head. A banner with the word 'Froome' followed by a question mark appears as cyclists take a bend. The French press label him a mutant; they say he can't possibly be that good at climbing. There are suspicions of his sudden bursting onto the scene: from a little-known rider on the verge of being dropped by his team, he came out of nowhere to take second place in the Vuelta a España in 2011.

It's a legacy that Froome and the other riders of his generation will have to overcome. Doping checks and regulations have tightened to an extent that it is now nigh on impossible to cheat. Froome deals with the accusations with characteristic dignity and politeness. He aims to be a role model for clean cycling.

Froome grew up in Kenya, where he used to ride through the townships and among wild animals, selling avocados off the back of his bike as an eight-year-old. 'Cycling was my freedom,' he says.

With three wins in the Tour de France, Froome has become the most successful British Grand Tour rider in history. His first victory took place at the historic 100th staging of the Tour, the year after he rode as *domestique* for Bradley Wiggins. The role of a *domestique* (French for 'servant') is to assist the team leader by providing a slipstream so they can save energy, carrying their water or supporting them in the bunch until the moment of attack. Consequently, the *domestiques* are largely unknown figures, often sacrificing all for the team, peeling off before the finish line after having spent everything they had. Yet despite riding essentially on behalf of someone else, in the 2012 Tour, Froome came second.

Those crowds that line the route of the Tour give so much to the riders, a much-needed cheer of encouragement, a turbo-boosting Mexican wave, sometimes even a gentle push. It is one of the curiosities of the Tour, these crowds that spill into the road, parting at the last moment. 'We have a unique sport; it is a privilege to be able to get up close to the race and to the event,' says Brian Cookson, UCI president. 'But people have a responsibility to respect that as well.' It's what led to the punching of Eddy Merckx; it means those keen photographers whose desire to get a close-up often results in their camera, and the rider, smashing to the ground. An ascent in the 2016 Tour saw a fan attempting to run alongside the riders, cape flowing behind him. He received a jab in the face from Froome.

Poor weather on the ascent up Mont Ventoux convinced the organisers to bring the finish line a short way down the mountain, displacing the crowds from that top section and squeezing them into spaces already over-filled with fans. Those groups that spill into the road spilled too far and the lead motorbike had to stop, causing Froome to crash into him. A second motorbike hit from behind and broke his frame. With his support car 5 minutes back, he began to run, cleated shoes slipping on the tarmac. There's no rule stating that you're not allowed to run – as long as you cross the finish line with a bike. He was finally given one, and retained the yellow jersey.

Perhaps Froome will be the first to legitimately break the five-win record. 'I don't see anyone beating Chris Froome for the next few years,' said Merckx.

CHAPTER THREE

WONDER WOMEN

Alfonsina Strada – Riding with the men

Don't be a fright.
Don't attempt a 'century'.
Don't refuse assistance up a hill.
Don't go without a needle, thread and thimble.
Don't appear in public until you
have learned to ride well.
Don't undertake a long ride if you are not
confident of performing it easily.

From a list of 'don'ts' for women cyclists
published in the *New York World*, 1895

The 1924 Giro d'Italia nearly didn't happen. The multiple-stage race through the mountains and landscapes of Italy had been staged almost every year since its launch in 1909, but a dispute over pay in 1924 led to a boycott by many of its top riders. In a post-war era, staging races was difficult, though vital in restoring morale and boosting the economy, but without a full complement of participants, the race wouldn't go ahead. The organisers opened up the field to anyone who wanted to enter and Alfonsin Strada signed up.

Alfonsin was in fact Alfonsina, a woman – while the rules didn't strictly exclude female entrants, it was highly unusual for ladies to compete. Whether the organisers knew she was not a man and allowed her anyway or whether they genuinely didn't realise until it was too late, she lined up at the start line in her black woollen shorts, black socks and short black bobbed hair.

Growing up as a peasant girl in rural Italy, it had felt like a miraculous day when Alfonsina's father had returned home from work with a bicycle that he'd traded for some chickens. Alfonsina was entranced and quickly learned how to ride – she had found a way to break free from the poverty of farm life.

However, it was improper for a girl to ride a bike; people teased her, men made unwanted advances and others treated her as if she were insane. In her town she became known as the 'Devil in a Dress'. Her cycling brought shame upon her family so they forbade her to continue. But Alfonsina was determined not to give up her passion. She would tell her mother she was going to Mass, but instead would ride to the next town to compete in a race.

Her first win came when she was just 13, and her prize was a pig. She proceeded to win nearly all the girls' races she entered, and often also the boys'. An invitation to race the Grand Prix of St Petersburg followed – highly unusual for a woman – and at the age of 18, she twice raced the

Giro Lombardia, the second time finishing ahead of many men. Her mother was desperate for her to marry, become a seamstress and leave all this cycling nonsense behind, so she was thrilled when she found a suitor, Luigi Strada – until it transpired that he was also a cycling enthusiast. They married in 1915 and moved to Milan, where Luigi coached her on the velodrome.

The 1924 Giro began with a 300 km stage from Milan to Genoa; after stage two – a 310 km ride to Florence – Alfonsina was in 56th place out of 90 entrants, and she had caught the attention of the press. The organisers realised that her inclusion would boost the popularity of the race: the spectators loved her. One newspaper reported that:

> *In only two stages this little lady's popularity has become greater than all the missing champions put together.*

By the end of the third stage, one-third of the field had dropped out; Alfonsina had become the race heroine.

In stage 7, a 305 km mountain stage from Foggia to L'Aquila, the weather turned. Roads turned to mud, their stony surfaces slick with the downpour, and riders made the brutal journey through the Sirente–Velino mountains with descents made treacherous by horizontal wind and rain. Alfonsina fell, limping into L'Aquila with bruised bones and swollen joints. The following stage was no easier: more mountain climbs and impassable roads led to many more riders abandoning the race; Alfonsina had several punctures and suffered a terrible crash which broke her handlebars in two. The heroine's race seemed over. A local farm woman came to her rescue, giving her the handle from her broom to use instead. But it was too late: she had missed the cut-off time for the stage. Alfonsina was disqualified.

Such was the support she received from the public that the organisers allowed her to continue, though she could no longer officially be part of the race. Emilio Colombo, the editor of *La Gazzetta dello Sport*, the magazine which sponsored the race, arranged to pay her continued food, board and massage out of his own pocket.

She finished her next stage 25 minutes past the cut-off time, but the spectators had all stayed, waiting to see this exceptional woman. She was flat-out with exhaustion, hungry and in tears, but the crowd lifted her from her bike and carried her through the air, giving her the reception of a champion. It was the boost she needed; her renewed determination took her to Milan, where she finished the race – all 3,613 km of it – arriving to a hero's welcome and a prize of 50,000 lire raised by the public. Only 35 riders of the original 90 completed the race. By reaching Milan, Alfonsina had earned the respect and affection of her fellow competitors and the public.

She continued to race, notching up 36 victories in a long career, but she would never ride in the Giro again. The following year, the pay dispute was over and the champions were back. Her previous benefactors turned their backs; the organisers refused her entry. No female competitors would ever again race in a Grand Tour. Yet Alfonsina had been, and would always be, the woman who rode with the men.

Eileen Sheridan – The Mighty Atom

[She] rocked the racing world, setting up
completely new standards for women's records.

THE BICYCLE

The ride from Land's End to John o'Groats is the most iconic in the British Isles; from the bottom left-hand corner of England to the top right-hand corner of Scotland, the 'End to End' ride extends 870 miles through steadily morphing landscapes, stretching from the devilish Cornish hills to the vast Scottish mountain ranges. It's the most popular long-distance challenge in the UK, and it typically takes touring cyclists between ten and 14 days to complete the distance. In 1954 Eileen Sheridan rode it in two days, 11 hours and 7 minutes.

It was a blustery, overcast day in June when Eileen set out, and the weather only grew worse as she travelled northwards, nearing Scotland in high winds and torrential rain. Fuelled by blackcurrant juice, soup, sugar and chicken legs, she rode day and night, taking few breaks and supported by her team, who supplied her with food and drink and eventually had to feed her when her numb fingers could no longer hold knife and fork. 'It just went on, and on, and you felt that you were never going to get there,' she said. With blistered hands, she reached John o'Groats, sleep-deprived, fatigued and with a new women's record.

It was the most gruelling ride in a career that saw Sheridan break every single one of the 21 professional long-distance and place-to-place records on the books of the Women's Road Records Association.

Joining Coventry Cycle Club with her husband Ken, it had never been Eileen's intention to race. Touring and club runs were more her thing: 'That's where the club spirit is found,' she said. Nonetheless, in 1944 she entered an informal 10 mile time trial; her approach was so nonchalant that she turned up without the required racing kit and a fellow club member had to lend her his. Much to everyone's surprise, including her own, she finished in 28 minutes 30 seconds – a new club record.

A year later she formally entered a 25 mile event run by the Birmingham Time Trial Association. Again, she set a club record. The Yorkshire Federation 12-hour time trial in 1949 was her first big event, though she nearly didn't go, as money was tight and travelling with a team to Yorkshire was expensive. Several of her clubmates at Coventry CC put the funds together, keen to see what 'their Eileen' could achieve. She rode 237.32 miles, breaking the previous record by 17 miles – a distance that would have earned her fifth place in the men's race.

She began taking all the distance records: the 30-mile in 1948, the 50-mile in 1949 and the newly introduced 100-mile in 1950, which Eileen won in 4h 37m 53s. Nothing would stop her riding, not even the birth of her son: she was back in the saddle seven weeks afterwards and winning races again within five months. Many of her records came within touching distance of the men's. The nation sat up and took notice – here was a woman who was proving again and again how capable the 'weaker' sex could be. Her diminutive and feminine appearance belied her strength and endeared her to the public; she seemed a regular housewife, not the powerhouse rider one might expect. The press labelled her the 'Mighty Atom'.

Time trialling was the dominant sport of British road riding in those days, in contrast to the bunch-style racing favoured on the Continent. This style of racing suited Sheridan, who was never faster than when she had someone to chase:

> No one ever passed me in time trials. I loved the thrill of chasing... I just had to try hard and win.

It was only a matter of time before she attracted the attention of sponsors, and in 1951 Hercules Cycle Company gave her a three-year contract to promote their business by breaking records.

She spent those three years steadily demolishing the existing times. 'Record breaking was a lonely business,' she said, just her and the tarmac, her support crew in the Hercules van pacing her as she rode her way through the list: London to York, to Cardiff, to Edinburgh, to Birmingham, to Brighton and back – 25 miles, 50 miles, 100 miles, 12 hours, 24 hours. After that Land's End to John o'Groats ride, Eileen had gone on to ride a further 130 miles, fighting hallucinations and exhaustion to take the 1,000 mile record. Her time of three days and 1 hour remained unbeaten for 48 years. Five of her records still stand.

Her final record was in 1954: the 25-mile time trial, her least favourite – she claimed it took her that long just to warm up. After two attempts, she secured the record, and with that, she retired – there were no records left to break.

Beryl Burton – Northern soul

*She just had her own ideas of what she
was going to do and she did it.*
DENISE BURTON-COLE, BERYL'S DAUGHTER

Every so often there comes along a truly remarkable figure,
whose brilliance earns them a place in history. In the 1960s,
this was Beryl Burton.

A sickly child, Burton was told never to exercise – she
had heart arrhythmia and was hospitalised aged ten with
rheumatic fever. It wasn't until her husband Charlie
suggested she come along to his cycle club as a way to
improve her health that she took it up, riding around the
local Yorkshire countryside. For her first few rides, she
would conceal her struggles, embarrassed that she couldn't
keep up with the others, but after a while she began to sit
comfortably within the pack and was soon leaving the rest
of them behind.

Road time trials had been the staple of British cycling
since the late 1800s, when massed sprints had been banned
for being too dangerous. Over distances of 25, 50 and 100
miles, individuals would race against the clock and it was
in these events that Beryl dominated, obliterating the field.
Dedicated, determined and bloody-minded, she never
slowed down. The Best All-Rounder award was given to the
rider with the best average score from all of their events over
the course of a year. Beryl was crowned the winner every
single year between 1959 and 1983.

An amateur throughout her career, she stayed at the
top through sheer determination. Training runs would

take place in the evenings, at weekends, slotted into gaps between working and raising her daughter, Denise. The family was never wealthy; before they could afford a car, Beryl would cycle to her races, arranging a rendezvous part-way back with husband Charlie, who would ride to meet her with Denise in a child seat. There was no money for the luxury of a track bike; Beryl had just one bicycle that she used for her races on both road and track, switching over the wheels and sprockets as necessary. Her first set of track wheels had been bought for 30 shillings ahead of the 1959 pursuit World Championships, but they were cracked around the spoke holes and she was refused entry to the race. A fellow competitor came to her aid, lending her a set of wheels, and Beryl went on to take the gold and her first world title.

This was the decade in which the ladies at the Ford plant in Dagenham fought for recognition of their skills; pay was far from equal, it was illegal for women to take the contraceptive pill and in the USA women were not permitted to get a credit card in their name. The perception that women were less capable than men was no exception in the world of cycling. At the height of her career, whenever Beryl told people that she was a cyclist, they would say, 'Oh, take it very steady. If the hills get too hard you must get off and walk. I'm sure the boys will wait for you.'

But time and again she proved she was stronger than 'the boys'. In open events she would consistently beat top class male riders, passing her fellow competitors with, 'Eh, lad, you're not trying!' In the 12-hour time trial of 1967 she cycled 277.25 miles, beating her rival Mike McNamara and giving him a Liquorice Allsort from her jersey pocket as she passed. He took it with a 'Ta, love!' and Beryl went on to set the record. It was two years before a man beat her distance; no woman has ever bettered it.

Following in her mother's tracks, Denise also became a top cyclist. Many times mother and daughter would stand side by side on the podium; together they set a record for the women's 10 mile tandem time trial. But these races weren't without rivalry: in one race, after Beryl had set the pace throughout, Denise zipped past her on the line. Beryl refused to shake her daughter's hand on the podium and wouldn't let her in the car afterwards, making her cycle home. 'I just felt Denise hadn't done her whack.'

Even as Beryl grew older, she refused to give up, continuing through illness and injury, her blind determination and sheer force of will keeping her winning titles well into her forties. Doctors advised her to take it easy; friends begged her to scale things back, but she would murmur about having 'just this race and just that race to do'. At the age of 41 she was hit by a car, breaking her shoulder blade and her leg. 'Most 41-year-olds would have retired at that point,' writes Jim McGurn, who interviewed Beryl when she was 45. 'Beryl, however, launched herself into a physiotherapy programme, was walking in three months, and, within six months of the accident, won the National 10 mile Time Trail Championship.'

She died the day before her 59th birthday while out delivering invitations to the party. After a lifetime of pushing herself to the absolute limit, her heart just stopped. It was a sudden and shocking loss, but in the end she had been doing what she loved: riding her bike.

Eileen Gray – Championing women's cycling

I was really shy as a young girl. Timid and very
mousy. And I probably would have stayed that way
had it not been for this old bike that I was given
during the war. It changed me from that shy young
woman into the confident person that I became...
It sort of opened the way for me I suppose.

Eileen Gray began cycling when a rail strike forced her to commute by bike. Riding through the war-torn streets of London, from Dulwich to the Harrow Road, she discovered the freedom and joy of cycling. A passion was born and she began searching around for a cycling club in the local area. Only one, the Apollo Cycling Club, accepted women.

Her first and only international event was in 1946, when Gray and two teammates were invited to take part in a race in Denmark. The trio completely trounced the Danish opposition who, it turned out, were a theatre troupe who rode bicycles as part of their act. The organisers had merely thought to stage an entertaining side-show, a novelty race as part of the more serious men's events. Gray determined to fight for women's cycling to be taken seriously.

Following the birth of her son the next year, Gray retired from riding but would dedicate the rest of her life to ensuring women's cycling was given equal opportunity to men's.

Founding the Women's Track Racing Association in 1949, which later became the Women's Cycle Racing Association, she began working internationally to stage women's races. It was an uphill battle. 'The French were up for it, as were the Belgians, but surprisingly it was the Dutch who were very much against women racing,' said Gray. 'The Swiss and Italians weren't very helpful either.'

In 1954 the National Cycling Union 'forgot' to table their motion at the UCI (the world governing body for sports cycling) conference asking for women's records to be recognised. But the following year, the motion was tabled, and passed. Gray had secured a breakthrough: women's records would receive official UCI accreditation.

In 1955 the first official UCI 500 m women's race took place at Herne Hill velodrome, in south London. Daisy Franks became the first ever female world record holder. The event was a triumph – even though they did have to stitch their own sandbags to ensure the track adhered to international race rules.

In the same year the British women's team received an invitation from the French to enter a three-day stage race at Roanne. Said Gray, 'They beat the French easily, which I don't think had been in the French plan.' The subsequent publicity gave a huge boost to women's cycling and in 1958, after 11 years of hard work and sustained effort on Gray's part, France hosted the first ever women's World Championship road race.

Opposition was still encountered from many quarters. Celebrated Olympic cyclist Reg Harris ensured that women were banned from one track and some men refused to recognise their achievements. In the 1960 event in Leipzig, the women's team were given £100 by the NCU and expected to cover the rest of their expenses themselves. When their race was called, they found that their entire set of spare tyres and tubes had been 'cleared away' by a colleague after the conclusion of the men's race – spares that they had paid for with their own money. Gray viewed it as sabotage.

The NCU was replaced by the British Cycling Federation in 1959 and Gray served as its president from 1976 to 1986, during which time she pushed for women's cycling to be included in the Olympics. In 1984 this was finally achieved: 45 women lined up for the road race at the Los Angeles Olympics, representing 16 nations.

Today, women's cycling still has a long way to go, with lack of sponsorship, limited media coverage, unequal pay and disparity in status still holding the sport back. But Eileen Gray's legacy is clear: in Rio 2016, riders from around the world took part in cycling events over four disciplines – track, road, BMX and mountain bike – and in every one there was a race for women.

Marianne Martin – Winner of the first
Tour de France Féminin

It wasn't about the money anyway.
We did it because we loved it.

When Marianne Martin's father offered her money as a graduation gift, she said, 'Great – I can buy a racing bicycle.' So he withdrew the offer and bought her a camera instead. In 1980s America, competitive women's cycling was not really the thing.

Marianne had raced throughout her time at college, discovering an aptitude for climbing, and winning many of the races she entered. Her first national race was the Tour of Texas; she'd called in sick from work in order to compete and then ended up winning. With her picture in the paper she 'got totally busted'.

In 1984, the organisers of the Tour de France announced an event for women, the Tour de France Féminin. There would be 18 stages compared to the men's 23, with 1,080 km covered as opposed to 4,000 km. But the race would run concurrently with the men's, on the same course, with all the climbs, and the same finishing lines. The women would ride ahead and finish their race around 30 minutes before the men. Huge crowds would be there to cheer them on.

Marianne was desperate to ride in the Tour. She had missed out on team selection for the 1984 Olympics, but felt that she was just finding her form and would be good enough. She drove to Colorado to speak to the national cycling coach, Edward Borysewicz, trying to convince him to let her on the team. 'Believe me, Eddie, you won't be disappointed,' were her parting words; she was given the last spot on the team a few weeks before the Tour was due to begin.

Six teams of 36 women lined up at the start. Marianne finished the first stage in third place, with two Dutch riders ahead of her. It was a surprise to everyone – the Americans were largely unknown, and even within the team, Marianne wasn't thought to be the best rider.

Stage 12 took the riders into the Alps, with two mountain passes. Marianne knew she could climb and was desperate to earn the polka dot jersey. Early in the stage, she made a breakaway, finding herself alone for the majority of the 45 miles. Her gamble worked. 'I raced ahead because I wanted that jersey and when I got to the top of the hill, I was 10 minutes ahead of the next riders.' She won the stage and was placed second overall: 1 min 4 sec behind the race leader.

Rather than merely providing a sideshow to the men's event, the women's race was proving a huge success. The crowds loved them; the world's media were forced to sit up and take notice. Following Marianne's success in the mountain stage, *The New York Times* finally ran a story. One photographer reported:

> *I got a sense that the women were having more fun than the men – there was less pressure on them.*

Marianne took the leader's yellow jersey after stage 14. The team knew their job was now to keep Marianne in yellow. 'It was just exhilarating. This was the best race in the world and we were winning.'

The team went into the final stage with a comfortable lead, crossing the finish line to ecstatic cheers from the crowd. Marianne and the men's winner, Laurent Fignon, stood side by side on the podium to receive their trophies. Marianne was awarded $1,000, which she shared with the team. Fignon took away prizes worth upwards of $100,000.

Funding and support dwindled in the following years, and there was no race in 1990 or 1991. When it returned, the race was no longer staged concurrently, and in 1998 was renamed La Grande Boucle Féminine. Over time the race shrank, with fewer days, shorter stages, and in some years no race at all. By 2009, La Grande Boucle had become a four-day race, causing eventual winner Brit Emma Pooley to call it 'more of a petite boucle'. Then it stopped for good. In 2016 it was reintroduced – as a one-day race called La Course.

Marianne retired from cycling, taking on two jobs to repay the debts she had incurred while racing and riding in the Tour de France. But she had no regrets.

> *Even if I hadn't won, so what? I got to race my bike every day, I was fed and got massages every day. And I was in France. To me, that was the greatest thing in the world.*

Jeannie Longo – In it for the long haul

*I swear I won't go on, and then I find
I manage to keep as fit as ever.*

An odyssey of longevity – if not the greatest female cyclist of all time, then the most tenacious – Jeannie Longo was among those who lined up at the first ever women's road race in the 1984 Olympics in Los Angeles. Proceeding to race in every single Olympic Games for the next two decades, her final appearance was at Beijing in 2008; she had begun her Olympic career before some of her competitors in that race had even been born.

For 35 years, the sight of Jeannie Longo was a familiar one, seemingly never missing from the peloton and rarely absent from the podium. Her unruly dark curls grew streaked with grey and her sun-lashed skin told tales of the passing years, but never did she seem to run out of energy. 'When I started racing, she was dominating the sport, and she still dominates it,' said three-time Tour de France winner, American Greg LeMond in 2002.

Longo was indeed a remarkable cyclist. She won every available title in her sport: world champion 13 times in track and road; Olympic medallist four times; three-time winner of the women's Tour de France; and French national champion an incredible 59 times. Trophies fill her house. A versatile rider, she also won medals in mountain biking. She set the Hour record a total of six times.

But she was as much criticised as she was celebrated; she annoyed her teammates, and was once banned from the team for selfish tactics. She was known for doing things her own way and giving short shrift to anyone who would tell her otherwise. Paranoid, she would keep her bike in her room rather than leave it with the team mechanics. Systems and rules mean little to Longo; she fell out with the French cycling federation many times, threatening to change citizenship, and even suing them following accusations of missed drugs tests. The peloton was not a place for making friends. 'Many cyclists don't like her because when she loses, she never praises the winner,' said French sports journalist André-Arnaud Fourny. 'She lacks respect for them as riders,' said Canadian cyclist Genny Brunet. 'She's as unforgiving of other people's mistakes as she would be of her own.'

For the sake of her bicycle, Longo sacrificed motherhood; cycling was the only thing she cared about. It took her away from the trappings of social convention; through the sport, she attained what she never could have achieved with a 'normal' life. But inevitably, she found herself snared by the very thing that had once freed her. She candidly admitted that she knew only how to ride. She became a prisoner of cycling, caught in its web. 'I invested myself so heavily into cycling that there were other things I never did.'

After three decades at the top of the sport, her extraordinary career came to an end, though under a cloud of suspicion after her husband and coach was arrested for buying the banned oxygen-boosting drug EPO. Whether or not it was ever intended for Longo, French national coach Francis Coquoz summed it up when he said: 'When you speak of French women's sport, you speak of Jeannie Longo. She is a monument.'

Marianne Vos – The Cannibal (mark II)

I'm a cyclist, I love cycling more than anything.

She has often been referred to as a female Eddy Merckx, her hunger, power and desire to win taking her from six times Dutch junior champion to being renowned as the greatest cyclist in the world. Tougher and stronger than anyone else, she dominates each race she enters, forcing the rest of the field to respond to her power and raise their game to match hers. Being the best of the rest behind Marianne is as good as it gets – it's not very often that you get to beat her.

Lizzie Armitstead nearly did, in London 2012, the roads slick with rain as they often are in the British summer. Vos and Armitstead had formed a breakaway in the descent from Box Hill – together with Shelley Olds of the USA and Russian Olga Zabelinksaya – a 30-mile sprint back to The Mall where one of them would be crowned Olympic Champion. But Olds punctured and Zabelinksaya struggled to pull her weight; 20 km from the finish, she was dropped. The race had as much drama as any: terrible weather, terrific climbing, super-fast sprints and a nail-biting finish as the two remaining leaders surged towards the line. Lizzie put her head down and gave it everything she had. But it's rarely that someone out-sprints Vos, *Vosje*, the Cunning Little Fox. The Dutch superwoman took it on the line, a bike's length clear.

A versatile sportswoman, she has Olympic medals in road and track, and world titles across three disciplines: track, road and cyclo-cross. She gained her first world title aged just 19, and in 2013 she took her fifth World Championship in a row, won the Tour of Flanders and sprinted across the line in the world road race, 15 seconds ahead of her nearest rivals.

A shy girl, she took up cycling so that people would notice her, to make a name for herself. Her name is certainly well-known now.

> *Winning feels so good and gives such a positive boost. Seeking that feeling has become a real addiction.*

In 2014 a hamstring injury forced her to take an extended break. She had been overtraining, pushing her body to the point beyond where it would recover. She spent her downtime promoting initiatives to encourage women to ride.

It would be easy for her to rely on her natural talent to climb and sprint, but she knows that much of the race is psychological — how much can you force your body to cope with? It's not just about winning; it's about the determination to reach the finish line.

> *I think I'm suffering, but for sure the others are also. You don't know how much pain they're in compared to me. And can you go through*

the pain? I'm always asking myself these questions. Somewhere, you stop. But where do you stop? And, of course you can push yourself really far, but at one point, you will stop before you fall off your bike dead. But how far can you go...?

Kristin Armstrong – The woman who just won't quit

Working and being a mom has been my secret weapon. It provides my balance and it keeps me on track and it keeps me super focussed.

At the 2016 Olympic Games in Rio, Kristin Armstrong took gold for the USA in the time trial, a few days before her forty-third birthday. In doing so she became the first cyclist, male or female, to win three consecutive gold medals in the same discipline.

Kristin's road to the top hasn't been easy. A successful triathlete, she was forced to retire from the sport because osteoarthritis in her hips made it too painful to run. So she focussed on cycling, excelling at time trial and road, and became National Road Race champion in 2004 and Time Trial champion the following year. The Olympics in Beijing beckoned, but Kristin was unsure whether she was in a financial position to compete – while men can easily live off their winnings, there's little money in women's cycling. She moved in with her boyfriend so that she could afford to keep training. ('Don't tell him that!' she commented. The pair are now married.)

She stormed the time trial in 2008, coming 25 seconds ahead of second-place Brit Emma Pooley. Crowned World Time Trial champion in 2009 for the second time, and at the top of her game, she retired to have a child.

However, the buzz of racing proved too great to resist, so Kristin made the decision to return to cycling, hoping to make the 2012 Olympics. But a crash in the 2012 Exergy time trials meant a broken collarbone, which put her selection for London in doubt. In the medical tent, she could picture the next day's headlines: *Kristin Armstrong crashes out of Olympic squad*. The media's influence on the sport was substantial; a story like that might sway the selection committee. Kristin knew she deserved a place on that squad so with the help of her doctor, she strapped herself up and appeared to the cameras, hiding the pain behind her smile, asserting her fitness. She made the squad and in the time trial at the London Olympics, she took gold.

Hip surgery meant she retired for the second time in 2013. It really looked as if her career was over, and she returned to her regular life of being a mother and holding down a job. But with Rio on the horizon, she made the decision to give it one more shot. 'Something keeps driving me back… I love challenges in life.' The cycling wasn't the only challenge: she had no sponsorship deals and no commercial endorsement. An arbitration hearing put forward by two athletes who believed they should have gone to Rio meant that she could have been dropped from the team. She also faced constant questions from the media about her age and her suitability to remain in the sport. 'You're a mom and a boss. Why keep doing it?' Her reply? 'Because I can.'

The time trial course at Rio 2016 was slippery with rain. Setting off at intervals from the other competitors, Kristin gave chase. She averaged nearly 25 mph throughout the 29 km course, a strong performance that steadily closed the lead. When her coach radioed her to tell her that she was in the medals, she found an extra burst of energy to ensure it was gold.

Time will tell if Rio will prove to be her final Olympics, but what a career to have – each time leaving the sport while at the top.

'For so long we've been told that we should be finished at a certain age. And there are a lot of athletes out there that are actually showing that that's not true. For all the moms out there, I hope that this was a very inspiring day.'

CHAPTER FOUR
BEYOND THE BIKE

Karen Darke – A born adventurer

*It is amazing to think that not that many
years ago the treatment of paraplegics was
generally regarded as a waste of time.*
HRH PRINCE CHARLES

With a website full of photos of extraordinary things and extraordinary places, Karen Darke's life is a catalogue of adventures and expeditions beyond many people's wildest dreams. What is most remarkable about Karen is that she has no mobility in her lower body: everything she does – handcycling, skiing or climbing – relies on upper body strength. Small, blonde and powerful, she smiles in the face of adversity.

Karen has a self-professed addiction to mountains, wilderness and adventuring – an addiction that saw her, as an able-bodied teenager, climb the Alpine peaks of Mont Blanc and the Matterhorn, the 'mountain of mountains'. Aged 20 she won the KIMM mountain marathon: two days of self-supported racing and route-finding through the Swiss Alps. Then, at age 21, on a climbing expedition she fell 10 m from a cliff, breaking her neck. She was paralysed from the chest down.

At first, Karen thought that she would have to give up her active lifestyle – her recovery was dominated by questions of 'how?', the logistics of assisted expeditions so much harder, the cost of equipment so much higher. To abandon that life, to accept that it was all over, would have been the easy option. Persisting with it seemed impossible.

But Karen was an adventurer through and through – giving up her life of exploration was a worse prospect.

> I realised I didn't have a choice. I'm wired how I'm wired and I can't change that, regardless of the fact I can't walk. I like feeling my blood pump, the elements shape me, being outdoors... I was still me, just with a different operating mode.

So she explored those other ways of operating, focussing on what she could do, rather than on what she couldn't. Four years after her accident she travelled 1,000 miles across Central Asia and over the Himalayas on a recumbent three-wheeled hand-cranked bike. Back in the mountains – exploring, independent and surrounded by landscapes of astounding beauty – Karen felt herself again.

A decade of adventuring followed, where no part of the world was off-limits. Through dense forest and volcanic mountain ranges she handbiked the length of Japan; a three-month kayaking expedition saw her traverse the Inside Passage along the archipelago-strewn Pacific coast of Canada and Alaska. In sub-zero temperatures she sit-skied the massive ice sheets of Greenland; under a hot sun she circumnavigated the Mediterranean island of Corsica by sea kayak. The following year she scaled the sheer sides of El Capitan in Yosemite Valley.

The life of an athlete beckoned, and in 2009 Karen became a bronze medallist at the Para-Cycling World Cup, joining the British Paralympic team the following year. It was a lifestyle that suited her, the routine of daily training and the fitness that comes with it a satisfactory alternative to the thrill of exploring. A lifetime of adventuring, of pushing her limits, had developed in her a toughness that would give her the edge as an athlete: an insight into the limits of the human psyche and a knowledge that when things got really hard, when the pain was almost too much to bear, she could dig that little bit deeper and survive.

Her achievements over the next seven years included medals of every colour in Paralympics and World Championships, in handbike and triathlon. The 2012 London Paralympic Games were her first and she won silver in the road time trial, hoping to add another medal in the road race. Medals are what matter, after all: the reward, the prize money, the proving to sponsors and team bosses that they made the right selection. The race had played out well; she rounded the final corner in bronze medal position, ready to sprint to the line. But it would be her teammate, friend and training partner Rachel Morris that she would be sprinting against. She could have pushed ahead, battled it out for that all-important podium, to make the years and months of training, sacrifice and pain worth it. But she didn't want to take that away from her teammate. With 50 m to go, the pair drew level and crossed the finish line together, holding hands.

'Someone once said to me, "Disability is a state of mind not a state of body." That's a notion that relates to us all, regardless of whether we have a physical disability or not. Our own mind is our biggest obstacle to living and achieving our wildest aspirations.'

Sarah Storey – The swimmer turned Olympic cyclist

I started out in life not even realising the Paralympic Games existed. For me it's just sport.

It was almost accidentally that Sarah Storey became a cyclist. Sport had always been her thing, even though she was born with a non-functioning left hand after it became entangled in the umbilical cord. Always displaying a love for the outdoors and a passion for games, she would play netball and cricket in the back garden, not letting her disability hold her back: 'I just learned to catch with one hand before I learned to catch with two.' Watching the 1984 Los Angeles Olympics at six years old, she sat cross-legged in front of the TV, completely mesmerised, and dreamed of being an elite sportswoman. 'Seeing Sarah Hardcastle [the British swimmer] winning medals at those games, at the age of 15, I realised I could be old enough to do the same in 1992.' And she did: by the time Sarah was that age she had become a formidable swimmer, and took home six medals from the Barcelona games as part of Britain's Paralympics swimming team.

Her career went from strength to strength, but after three more Paralympics and three World Championships, an ear infection hit – and refused to go away. Sarah was advised to stay out of the pool for six weeks.

Unable to train, she was lent a bicycle to enable her to keep her fitness up. It would prove a seminal moment in her career: Sarah discovered a remarkable aptitude for cycling. With a little coaching and some dedicated training, she entered the British Cycling selection for the European Championships. Her time trial put her only 2 seconds behind the world record. She had broken it by the time she was given the all-clear to return to the pool.

Forced to choose between the two disciplines, her swimming coach helped her to make the decision: 'You have been 13 years on the British swimming team, won five Paralympic golds, six world titles, and set 60-odd world records. What more could you do?'

So Sarah became a cyclist, competing as a C5 athlete, where C means 'cycling' or riding a two-wheeled bicycle rather than a hand-cranked bike (H), a tricycle (T) or a tandem for visually impaired riders (B). The numbers 1–5 denote the grade of disability, where 5 is the least severe.

Despite having been a Paralympian for her entire career, Sarah worried that she wasn't a deserving Paralympic cyclist, and that her disability was not sufficient to warrant her inclusion.

> *I didn't want to be looked upon as a fraud. It took the coaches a while to convince me about the contribution your upper body makes in cycling, about how you need two hands for the bike handling, not to mention the braking.*

Her aptitude is such that she would often compete against able-bodied athletes, and win. Her first Paralympic cycling gold came in Beijing, in an individual pursuit time that would have put her in the top eight in the Olympic final. At the 2010 Commonwealth Games she became the first disabled cyclist to compete for England against non-disabled athletes. At a glance, it's easy to miss her disability, even though her left arm is 18 cm shorter than her right. 'You learn to balance really well, and over time it just looks natural.'

Inevitably, being on a bicycle can mean falling, and landing on the track is much harder than in the swimming pool. On two occasions Sarah has broken her collarbone, though that didn't stop her contesting and winning a world title before it had mended.

Winning the 3,000 m C5 individual pursuit in Rio 2016 gave Sarah her twelfth gold medal across the two disciplines and made her the most successful British Paralympian of the modern era, overtaking Baroness Tanni Grey-Thompson, who earned 11 medals during her career. Sarah's contributions to sport were recognised with an MBE in 1998, an OBE in 2009 and a Damehood in 2013.

It's a tough life being an athlete, especially a para-athlete, where perceptions are different and opinions are often influenced by a lack of understanding. Sarah has seen plenty of this, from comments questioning her legitimacy as a Paralympic cyclist to the time she was refused membership of her university swimming club because the coach 'didn't work with disabled athletes' – despite her being an international gold medallist.

> People get different things thrown at them in their lives. Challenges are personal. What one finds easy, another finds difficult. I am not brave or courageous. I am just an athlete.

Alex Zanardi – Changing gears

I see the human body as an incredible machine, totally undiscovered in many ways. Every one of us has a hidden tank of energy that comes out when needed.

London 2012. A Paralympian sits upright on the tarmac, his muscular torso perching on what remains of his amputated legs. His handcycle is held aloft in one mighty hand, high above his head in celebration of a gold medal-winning time trial. 'I've had a magical adventure – and this is a fantastic conclusion.'

Zanardi had begun his career as a Formula One racing driver: a hugely popular figure on and off the track, with an exuberant personality, a permanent smile and a penchant for performing doughnuts (making tyre mark circles) after a race. He had several world titles to his name and a lucrative contract when, in 2001, he lined up at the start of the IndyCar race at the Lausitz circuit in Germany. The race started well: with 13 laps to go, he had a solid lead. But coming out of the final pit stop, Zanardi lost control of his car, coming to rest side-on, directly in the path of the rest of the field. Moments later he was struck by another driver at a speed of over 200 mph. His car was ripped in two and Zanardi lost both legs.

With the arteries severed, he haemorrhaged a huge amount of blood. His heart had to be restarted seven times; his last rites were read on the helicopter ride to the hospital. Thankfully, quick action by his team and expert care by the doctors saved his life. Having chosen a sport involving potentially catastrophic consequences, he had often pondered the likelihood of such an accident and what he might do. 'I said I would probably kill myself.' But on waking up after his operation, the thought never crossed his mind. 'I was very happy, and full of joy at being alive.'

The process of rehabilitation can be a huge challenge: things don't magically change overnight, and that can be hard to deal with. Zanardi found his experience as a sportsman invaluable; his recovery was a slow, steady step-by-step process, in which he would set himself priorities and work towards them, building on what he had done the previous day – exactly as he would do when preparing for a race. It took one year to reach the stage where he could use his prosthetic legs efficiently – never in that time did he consider quitting sport.

> *Even in my hospital bed right after the accident, I knew I was mentally the same driver and athlete as I was before losing my legs.*

An invitation to speak and share his story at the New York marathon first sparked the idea of handcycling. Ever the sportsman, he thought that as he was attending, he might as well take part. A handcycle division had been introduced in 2000, so he learned how to ride. He came fourth after only four weeks of training.

There began a new passion, one that brought with it the thrill of competition and the benefit of fitness, as well as making use of a driver's knowledge of aerodynamics. This passion would lead to Zanardi joining the Italian handcycling Paralympic team and at the age of 45, against competitors in some cases half his age, racing to two gold medals and a silver.

The track used at the 2012 Paralympic games was Brands Hatch, the very same where Zanardi had raced as a driver. 'Last time I was here I was going about five times faster. With an engine pushing me I didn't realise it was so hilly.'

Many others come through difficulties and go on to achieve greatness, others who had in their turn inspired Zanardi.

'The perfect life is the combination of great moments and bad ones, and under that point of view, my life is fantastic, because I've certainly hit more than one bump.'

Megan Fisher – Beating the odds

*I truly believe we are all capable of
more than we know.*

Megan Fisher had always wanted to be an Olympian. From an early age she would daydream about being like sprinter

Flo-Jo or speed skater Bonnie Blair, but it was tennis that she loved the most. Together with her best friend Sarah Jackson, she taught tennis at a summer school in Chicago, the pair planning to share an apartment and go into teaching on their return to Montana. But on the road trip home they were involved in a horrific accident, a crash in which their car rolled eight times. Tragically, Sarah lost her life. The impact crushed Megan's leg and left her in a coma.

Megan awoke to an uncertain future: overcome with grief, and having suffered severe brain trauma, it took time for her to come around to the realities of her new life. In that time, she had two amputations on her leg. Doctors tried to keep her expectations low, one medical professional sitting her down to tell her, 'Sweetheart, you'll never be as good as you were.'

It was her physical therapist who gave her the confidence to believe that she could lead a fulfilling life, free of pain. Less than a year after her second amputation, after having been told she'd never walk again, Megan completed her first triathlon. She had always resisted triathlon; it just seemed far too hard, but when crossing the finish line, the realisation hit home that her biggest obstacle was self-doubt. That one race proved that she could achieve anything she wanted; she could chase her wildest dreams.

Cycling had at first been an aid to mobility; struggling to walk, a bicycle had been vital to her getting out on her own. However, with tennis no longer a possibility, cycling became a natural choice for a competitive sport that Megan could take up – it had been the most enjoyable part of her triathlon. She joined cycling clubs and entered races, not classing herself as a para-cyclist – she wanted her fellow competitors to notice her missing leg only after she had passed them.

It took time to develop the strength and endurance to be successful in competition, but in 2010 she attracted the attention of Team USA and entered her first Paralympic Games in London 2012. She won gold.

It was an incredible journey from hospital bed to gold medal athlete and one that could, at any stage, have been dismissed as too difficult.

> *As an elite para-athlete I wish we could share our stories more often and inspire more people to challenge their own limitations.*

Indeed, for a para-athlete, the road to the top is more difficult than for many. In the face of negative or erroneous perceptions of people with disabilities, athletes battle to make their mark. There are countries that shame individuals with physical impairments and their athletes must overcome significant obstacles in order to represent their nations.

Even in the US, where attitudes towards disability are more open and a renewed obsession with cycling has swept the nation, para-cycling gets very little air time. 'A lot of the excitement, media attention, and support around the Olympics is not extended to the Paralympics,' says Megan.

Few Olympians can support themselves on their sport alone; for a Paralympian, it's nigh on impossible. The medical bills alone are astonishing: Megan paid $9,000 for a leg just to be able to walk around. As with most athletes, she must work in order to support her career, fitting training around her job. She even had to run a crowdfunding campaign just so that she could attend the trials for Rio.

Megan is living her childhood dream of representing Team USA on sport's grandest stage. 'I'm not disappointed that I'm not an Olympian. I'm more proud of being a Paralympian. That title is proof that I have had to overcome more than most to reach my dreams.' And to the doctor who told her she'd never again be as good as she once was, she says, 'I am proud to say that I am better than I ever was.'

Isabelle Clement – Wheels for Wellbeing

I constantly get asked, how fast can you go on this? I have no idea and I don't care. I don't cycle to keep up with the couriers. I cycle to exercise, to listen to birds, to feel happier.

It was trying to keep up with her four-year-old son that caused Isabelle Clement to turn her wheelchair into a bike – and open the door to a new life.

Isabelle had a spinal tumour at ten months of age, meaning that she has never been able to walk very far or run at all. When she reached her mid-twenties, she increasingly used a wheelchair to get about. She had once tried to learn to ride a bicycle as a child, but unable to balance or keep her feet on the pedals, she gave up the attempt. The lid closed on the idea of cycling. So when her son got his first bike, and Isabelle struggled to keep up, she began searching around and came across an adapter for her wheelchair. 'I realised cycling doesn't stop at the simple bicycle.'

The adapter has a large wheel at the front, powered by hand-cranks, which raises her wheelchair off its two small casters, making the ride smoother, faster and easier. Using hand-cranks also means she no longer gets mud up her arms.

Her first ride was a 'walk' with friends. With her transformed wheelchair, she left them behind. For the first time in her life, she felt the wind in her hair, the blood pumping round her veins and the whoosh of endorphins flooding her body. It was nothing like she had ever experienced before. That first ride was like crashing through a glass door – she had never envisaged travelling any distance at all under her own steam but suddenly, she could go as far as her imagination would take her.

Turning her wheelchair into a bike was a revelation. It wasn't just the travel; she also experienced a different attitude in those around her. No longer seen as 'someone in a wheelchair', she noticed how people reacted positively to her wheelchair bike: smiling, laughing and pointing in surprise. Their reaction is joy, not pity – even though she is exactly the same person, in exactly the same chair.

Isabelle took on the Directorship of Wheels for Wellbeing, a charity that maintains a fleet of bicycles, tricycles, tandems and wheelchair tandems to enable disabled people to access cycling. She also campaigns for better infrastructure for those with disabilities. 'Cycling infrastructure is built by people who assume disabled people don't cycle, and access is often poor,' she says. 'The assumption is that disabled people want to drive or need taxis to get about.' Some disabled cyclists are told: 'You can't cycle here. And anyway, if you were really disabled, you wouldn't be on a bike!'

Mobility is freedom, as Isabelle experienced with that first handbike ride. 'People don't realise how enabling and freeing the right set of wheels can be,' she explains. 'Powering my bike forwards is like powering my life forwards.'

Tara Llanes – The trail to recovery

How strange the earthquake must have seemed
to them, here where they lived so safely always!
They thought such a dreadful thing could happen
to others, but not to them. That is the way!
WILLIAM DEAN HOWELLS, *A SLEEP AND A FORGETTING*

Beautiful, charming and fearless, Tara Llanes (pronounced 'Yaw-ness') grew up riding bikes. Aged 11, she begged her mum to let her race BMX; then it was mountain biking, her indomitability leading her from race to race until she turned pro as a teenager. By the age of 30 she was regularly winning national and world titles, a popular, well-regarded figure on the MTB circuit. In 2007 she lined up to contest the final for a King of the Mountains event in Beaver Creek, Colorado; this had been where she'd first raced as a pro, 13 years previously. But Tara took a jump badly and was thrown over the handlebars, landing on her head and scorpioning onto her back, crunching her spine and her spinal cord. When she came round, legs lolling unmoving down the slope of the jump, panic took hold: 'I want to ride my bike again… Tell me I'm going to ride my bike again?'

It is the worst nightmare for those who chase the thrill of extreme sport, toying with danger, one misplaced wheel away from an irreversible life change. Bones heal; ligaments can be sewn. Damage the spinal cord and the body will never work in the same way again.

The next few years were a blur of trying to keep busy between occupational and physical therapy classes, learning to use a wheelchair, trying not to burn herself while cooking because she couldn't feel if she'd bumped into the stove, stretching, workouts in the pool, avoiding those long lonely moments when thoughts would run wild. In your head, you can be your own worst enemy. Your sense of self is hard to pin down – in one moment the path you thought you were on is blocked, and you have to work out what to do next. Standing is such a simple, unconscious thing. Who was Tara now she couldn't walk? What challenges would life hold now that standing up wasn't an option? Her relationship broke down. 'Is anybody ever going to want to date me?' Depression is an easy word to use, but it's more than that. It's the physical pain that buzzes below the surface almost all the time. It's the mental battle, the emotional issues that threaten to consume all.

While out in her wheelchair, people wouldn't see Tara the athlete, because it's hard to see beyond the chair; people approaching on the sidewalk would glance at her, unsure as to whether to keep looking or not.

It's the little things that give hope. Race for Tara was set up in the month after her accident by a father and son – people Tara didn't know, but who wanted to help in any way they could. The event helped to raise money for her medical bills; her insurance payout covered less than the cost of her wheelchair. That simple gesture by two strangers showed a kindness and generosity that helped to shape Tara's recovery. The race was intended as a one-off but it ran for seven years.

Some friends clubbed together to buy her a Sport-On Explorer bike: a three-wheel hand-pedalled dirt bike. At first she wasn't interested in riding it — it wouldn't be the same. But getting back out in the fresh air, powering her own vehicle and feeling the adrenaline rush that she had so missed, was the release she needed. She now has a company promoting and selling the bikes.

It's easy to look back and think, *If only*. But it was an accident, and that's what life throws at you sometimes.

> *I don't resent cycling. I love cycling – that's what I want to do the most, out of anything in the entire world.*

Taking those negatives and turning them into positives, Tara works as a consultant for a hotel chain who had once refused her assistance to get into the airport van. She campaigns for trail riding to be made accessible for the larger three-wheel bikes she now rides. In 2009 Tara was invited to train with the US Paraplegic Team at the Olympic Training Center in California. 'I was never invited when I raced mountain bikes, but I am now! Weird how things work, huh?!'

Tara is determined to walk again, even though she has been told that's impossible. It takes incredible mental strength to realise that, in the face of everything, life goes on.

'Funny thing is that as time went on and I went through loads of ups and down, depression, and then all time highs, I finally realized, who cares if I can't jump 25 ft gaps anymore? I love riding in the dirt and taking my Explorer and XCR out for a rip. All of these bikes allow me to feel my independence again and that is my freedom.'

Emmanuel Ofosu Yeboah – The one-legged cyclist

I saw before me a man determined to reverse the injustice of the disabled. A man who leads by example and who is not driven by self, but driven to help others.
KING OSAGYEFUO OF GHANA

Born without a tibia in his right leg in a country in which physical deformities are considered a curse, Emmanuel Ofosu Yeboah has been stigmatised his whole life. 'When you are a deformed child in Ghana, people think your mother sinned.' His father left rather than suffer the shame. Friends and family told his mother to poison her son or leave him by the river but she refused. She made sure that he had access to an education, carrying him the 2 miles to school each day – a school where he was the only disabled child. When he grew old enough to make the journey alone, he would hop.

When Emmanuel was 13, his mother fell sick. Against her wishes, he left school and went to Accra, the Ghanaian capital, where he could earn money to look after her. There, he was shocked to see disabled people everywhere, hundreds of them, begging. But he refused to do the same and instead began shining shoes for a meagre $2 per day. When his mother died, she told him, 'Don't let anybody put you down because of your disability.'

Her words had been a gift. Yeboah said:

> *I want to show everyone that physically challenged people can do something.*

Ten per cent of the population in Ghana is disabled: roughly two million people, all of them seen as lesser citizens. In the midst of the resigned depression of the beggars around him, Emmanuel made a plan: do something that would speak to both the able-bodied and the disabled, showing them that although he could only use one leg, he was just the same as everyone else – and just as capable. 'If you are a disabled person in your leg, you're not a disabled person in your mind.' He decided to ride a bicycle across Ghana.

Accepted for a grant from the California-based Challenged Athlete Foundation (CAF), Emmanuel was sent a bike and, in 2001, at the age of 24, he set off. Wearing a red T-shirt emblazoned with the words 'The Pozo' – Ghanaian slang for a disabled person – he cycled 380 miles across the nation. During his travels he spoke out against the government policy on disability and pushed for disabled people to be treated with the same respect as the able-bodied.

The bike ride elevated him to celebrity status. He returned with a mission to improve the lives of those with disabilities in Ghana. Invited to the King's palace, he became the first ever disabled person to be given permission to cross the threshold. In 2003 his right leg was amputated and replaced with a prosthetic – for the first time in his life he could walk, wear trousers and ride his bike two-legged.

A year later he founded the Emmanuel Education Fund to help disabled children attend school, donating upwards of 1,000 wheelchairs to those who were able only to crawl. In

2006, the Ghanaian Parliament passed a bill granting those with disabilities the same rights as are afforded to able-bodied citizens.

'In this world, we are not perfect. We can only do our best. I just want to make life better, and help people benefit from my experience.'

CHAPTER FIVE
THE LONG HAUL

Heinz Stücke – The most well-travelled man on Earth

I am on a treasure hunt. It is the bicycle that makes it all possible; the bike is my passport.

Why do we travel? To discover new places, to have new experiences, to expand our horizons. Through the miles accrued on the road, we challenge ourselves, feel free and find simplicity. It's an escape of sorts, and a dream that many harbour, to leave everything for a life-changing journey, to break free from the shackles of daily life and follow the road ahead, into the unknown, in search of adventure.

It's a dream that, for Heinz Stücke, became a reality the day he left his job as a tool and die maker, and began a journey that would not only be the journey of a lifetime, but would last a lifetime. It had been the simple call of the road, that call more attractive than the life towards which society would push him.

As a youth, he had spent some time travelling, returning to his hometown of Hövelhof, Germany, to take up his tools, thinking that he should settle down, find a wife, have children and do the things that were expected of him. But a year in the factory was as much as he could manage; his wanderlust had become irresistible. 'Why did I have to spend the rest of my life doing something that did not really interest me?'

So, at the age of 22, he left his home and, riding a blue steel three-speed bicycle, set off in search of the unknown. At first he rode with the simple motivation of discovering what was around the corner. Weeks turned to months, and his travels became a conscious attempt to avoid returning to the factory and his hometown – a community that seemed so small now his world had expanded so greatly. Eventually, his lifestyle gained a sense of permanence. The simplicity of living with a few basic necessities and the unhurried, clutter-free life of the open road were what kept him going. He felt a spark of excitement when crossing into a new country – a spark that never seemed to lose its brilliance, no matter how many borders he crossed. In the end, he crossed them all.

His bicycle had become his most treasured possession, his constant companion on the long road, a means to his adventure and a conversation starter. 'I am considered a good person because I ride a bike,' Stücke noticed. His vehicle was perceived as a non-threatening, approachable one, recognised worldwide and understood no matter the language. From the saddle he engaged people in conversation and made friends.

For money he would sell stories, pictures and a booklet with photos and narratives from his adventures. It takes a certain resilience to travel for so long, avoiding significant ties and relationships, as well as ignoring the call of home, whose draw is often hard to resist. 'Home is elsewhere,' Stücke would say. There were a number of 'hubs' in which he could recuperate or have things delivered, such as The Bunker in Paris and the home of his friend, Mr Lee, owner of the Flying Ball bike shop in Hong Kong.

Five decades were spent on the road, through ups and downs, and there were plenty of rough times. 'I had lots of brushes with death,' he said. He survived a hit-and-run in the Chilean desert, mobs chasing him in Haiti and a severe bee attack in Mozambique. He was robbed in the US by a man who'd given him a lift, detained by the Cameroon military and beaten by thieves in Cape Town. It was a fellow German passing in a car who saved him from near-death when a group of Freedom Fighters in Zambia held him at gunpoint; the driver heard Heinz pleading, 'I am a tourist!' after the gunmen had shot off his toe.

The world has changed since Stücke began his journey in 1962, as has he: that fresh-faced youth transformed into a world traveller — travels that filled 21 passports, man and bicycle ageing as the decades passed. His steed became patched with countless repairs, the top-tube rusting where sweat dripped from his nose and a second pair of handlebars added so he could avoid straining his neck. Stolen six times, it was returned on each occasion. In those 50 years he travelled through 196 countries and pedalled 648,000 km.

> *I had no idea the trip would last a lifetime. I happily kept postponing the return journey again and again – the urge to see another country was always stronger.*

But return he did, eventually, to Hövelhof, in a house donated by the town, which will be turned into a museum after his death. It is a vast treasure trove of mementos from the road, as Stücke is a collector, despite living what most would class as a minimalist life. For years he saved small strips from all the tyres he rode and he accrued dozens of hats. And then there are his diaries – expansive accounts of his travels, written on pages numbering over 18,000.

Many dream of freedom, though few truly experience it. It's difficult to chase those dreams – it means cutting ties with relations, family and friends, and being completely free. For most people, once the savings have run out, that means the end of the dream.

'Eventually, people wind up again where they started from. They get a good job. And then the woman comes, you know. And then they buy a house and then, maybe, children come. And then only the dream stays.'

Dervla Murphy – Travel pioneer

You never want your travelling to be too easy.

It was the beautiful simplicity of the bicycle as a means of travel that attracted Dervla Murphy. Ever since she had received a second-hand bike and an atlas for her tenth birthday, a wanderlust had gently lurked. While out riding and exploring the countryside near her home in southern Ireland, she would watch her spinning legs with the realisation: 'If I went on doing this for long enough I could get to India.'

Murphy is one of the most well-known and inspirational figures of cycle touring. Her travels are extensive and her books numerous. There is a simplicity to both her writing and her travelling, and therein lies her popularity: a genuine and gentle fascination with the world, coupled with a desire to discover more of it in as unobtrusive a way as possible. Lauded for her bravery, she maintains she's not brave – it's more an unassuming fatalism, accepting things as they come, rather than fearing the unknown: 'You're only courageous if you do something you're afraid of doing. If you're fearless there's nothing to overcome.'

Until the age of 30, Dervla lived at home, caring for her arthritic mother, taking any opportunity to tour around Ireland, Britain and Europe on her bike. By the time her mother passed away, shortly after her father's unexpected death, she had been 'like an elastic stretched to breaking point'. Freed from her domestic duties, in 1963 she set off, full tilt, for India.

It was an extraordinary thing for a shy country girl to attempt, given how little she knew of the world. Her luggage was basic: just one set of underwear, some woollen long johns and a .25 automatic pistol with four rounds of ammunition that she'd practised firing in the woods behind her house. With a bicycle stripped of its gears in order to make maintenance easier, she cycled out into one of the coldest winters in Europe for decades.

Perhaps it was her naivety that helped her to overcome the challenges of the road; instead of being afraid of what might lie in wait around the corner, she would simply ride, not wasting energy in worrying: 'What happens, happens.' And things certainly happened. Nearing Bulgaria, she was forced to dispatch a pack of wolves with her pistol, heart pumping with terror as the pack surrounded her, shooting the one on her shoulder as the others scarpered. The pistol helped to ward off unwelcome attention from men, too, though this happened very rarely – more often, a lone woman is perceived not as a threat but as someone to be protected.

Simplicity beckoned, a life where material possessions meant little and the only person to rely on was herself. 'The hardships and poverty of my youth had been a good apprenticeship for this form of travel.' Fiercely solitary, she discovered the value of travelling alone, able to establish relationships with local people naturally and easily. She always seemed to land on her feet, trusting in the unplanned nature of it all, finding hospitality in places where she was least expecting it. In seeking solitude she found kindness beyond her expectations.

From the bitter European winter she rode across Iran and Afghanistan, and after six months of cycling, she arrived to an Indian summer where her handlebars burned to the touch. Here was the focus of her long-held dream: the noise, the smells and the colours were overwhelming, all at once everything she had imagined – the first journey in what was to be a lifetime of travel.

By chance she met travel writer Penelope Betjeman in India, who encouraged her to visit a publisher on her return to London. When Dervla tied her battered old bicycle to the railings in an upmarket street in Mayfair, having cycled there from her home in Lismore, the publisher thought, *This is our kind of girl*.

Her subsequent travels have taken her to all corners of the world, either by bicycle or on foot, and sometimes with a pack animal. When her daughter Rachel was born, the pair travelled together, discovering ever more connection with the local community: 'Children pay little attention to racial or cultural differences [and] rapidly demolish barriers of shyness.' Confounding the notion that age should be a restriction, Dervla cycled 3,000 miles through Africa when she was 70.

'Be a light packer but a serious traveller,' Murphy advises, 'serious' meaning embracing the independence and solitude of the open road, keeping little contact with home and living appropriately to the place in which you find yourself. Travel should be slow-paced: not flashing above the beauty in an aeroplane, but feeling, smelling, tasting and touching it.

Scathing of technology, she writes by hand and by typewriter in her house in Ireland:

> *Everybody's been telling me for years that if I had a computer I wouldn't have to re-type all these pages – just press some mysterious mouse or rat or something and it would all come right.*

After a lifetime of relying on people's hospitality and goodwill, her travels have left her hopeful, as the world she knows is not the world that is shown in the headlines. There is an enduring goodness in people. For her, travel is not about the number of peaks climbed or the number of miles ridden, but how one's affection towards another race has grown. That is its purpose: to gain an insight into how others live, to discover different cultures and to learn from others.

And her advice to those who are afraid of taking the first step? 'Nothing dared, nothing gained.'

Richard and Nicholas Crane – Journey to the centre of the Earth

To travel hopefully is a better thing than to arrive, and the true success is to labour.
ROBERT LOUIS STEVENSON

Richard Crane and his cousin Nick were no strangers to adventure. Their combined expedition list totalled many thousands of miles, the more extreme the better: Richard had once run 2,000 miles through the Himalayas and together they had taken mountain bikes to the summit of Mount Kilimanjaro. Their latest mission was to journey to the place on the Earth's surface furthest from the open sea. No one had knowingly been there before – or even knew where it was.

In 1986 they set off from the Bay of Bengal on the Bangladeshi coast, cycling northwards for 5,300 km across India, Nepal, Tibet and China, towards the heart of Asia – the most remote place on Earth, bordered by the Gobi desert, the frozen wastes of Siberia and the Himalayas – in search of the point equidistant from the Arctic Ocean, the Yellow Sea in China and the Indian Ocean.

With only 50 days to travel 5,000 km, they envisaged a fast ride. They rode 20 lb Raleigh racing bikes specially made for them in the hectic days before their departure from London. Saying they travelled light would be an understatement.

With no tent, no change of clothes and no food, their weight-saving took on fanatical proportions: labels were snipped from clothes, chopsticks were cut in half and only the insert of ballpoint pens remained. Their toolkit consisted of one cone spanner, one tyre lever, puncture kit, a spoke tool and two Allen keys. In order to reduce weight even further they drilled holes in the spanner, cut the spoke tool in half and removed their front derailleurs – gears would be changed using fingers and heels.

It was an opportunists' expedition, completely reliant on the places and people they passed. Richard and Nick ate in roadside teahouses and stayed wherever they could find a bed; failing that, they slept in the open in their sleeping bags. Communication with the locals was achieved by miming.

Woefully unprepared for the changing weather or the state of the roads, they muddled through; in the first day alone they suffered sunstroke, extreme thirst, monsoon and near-hypothermia. Mountain passes of over 5,000 m led to altitude sickness, while temperatures ranged from 42°C to −10°C. But therein lay the journey's appeal. 'It was exactly what we had been seeking in adventure: problems we couldn't predict yet which we could survive.'

Yet the cycling, the weather and the domestic arrangements weren't their greatest difficulty: they attracted attention just by looking different and having shiny bicycles. Sometimes it was harmless – having 20 or 30 people watching them eat supper or get ready for bed – but at other times they were accused of being political activists or spies, and were arrested several times.

The closer they drew to the centre of the Earth, the more their target seemed to slip away. They had successfully traversed the Tibetan Plateau – possibly the first cyclists ever to do so – had followed the rough dirt track of the fabled Silk Road and they had survived the Gobi Desert. Finally, they reached Ürümqi, the settlement nearest to where they believed their destination to lie. Few roads led out of the town, its industrial sprawl surrounded by desert and oil fields. They took out the solar calculator that had been lugged from the Bay of Bengal and set about working out their destination. Locating the centre of the Earth required both interpretation of 'open sea' and some heavy-duty trigonometry, but at last they decided on a spot. Instead of 50 km, it was more like 500.

The area they were heading into was not permitted to tourists. However, they set out into the oil fields, hoping that two small men on bicycles would not be noticed. About 75 km from Ürümqi, they were picked up by the police, brought in and arrested yet again. It was impossible to explain their mission and protest their innocence to people whose language they didn't speak. They were eventually given a travel permit to Karamay, from where they could take a ride in a taxi and then ceremonially cycle the final few kilometres.

But the road was blocked by an irrigation ditch and the taxi driver refused to go on; the adventure was over. Richard and Nicholas begged: 'Please, we can ride our bikes from here, we can just go a little further; we will only be an hour.' The official turned a blind eye as they cycled alone into the desert.

Eventually, they came to the point they had identified: a bowl of sand, animal tracks, a hillock and sandstone rocks: the centre of the Earth. It had been an epic journey: they were thirsty, tired and well over their curfew, and would probably be arrested yet again by the search party that was, without doubt, already being formed.

But despite the sheer madness of their trip, the unlikely nature of it and the fairly unremarkable scene that greeted its end, despite their underlying sense of guilt at having broken the trust not only of the Chinese authorities but all the many hundreds of others who had provided shelter, sustenance and support throughout their journey, despite the physical struggles in a terrain far more arduous than they had imagined, their journey was a triumph: the thrill of doing something no one else has done before.

Turning their backs on the destination it had taken them so long to reach, they returned to the taxi, where the Head of Security was waiting for them. Back they went to the authorities at Ürümqi, where the pair humbly accepted responsibility for the whole trip and whatever might have gone wrong along the way. 'They accepted our apologies, came to congratulate us, organised our return tickets, and we parted the best of friends.'

Anne Mustoe – The improbable cyclist

It is by riding a bicycle that you learn the contours of a country best, since you have to sweat up the hills and coast down them.
Ernest Hemingway

It was a holiday in the winter of 1983 that changed Anne Mustoe's life. A successful headmistress, she was travelling through India as respite from a hectic autumn term when she saw a man riding a bicycle across the desert. 'I was seized with a sudden envy,' she said, the bicycle all at once seeming the best way to travel, the immediacy and intimacy of the experience something one couldn't get on a bus. 'I wanted to be out there myself, feeling the reality of India, not gazing at it through a pane of glass.' She made up her mind in that instant that she, too, would cycle across India – but why stop there? While she was at it, why not cycle around the world?

The decision surprised her friends; not particularly keen on the outdoors, she had never been one for camping, picnics or discomfort. It had been three decades since she had been on a bike. She was neither athletic nor young, and had no idea how to mend a puncture. Nearing retirement, she had a decent job, which she was good at and enjoyed.

It takes much courage to leave a secure and comfortable lifestyle, and for four years Anne's idea remained a dream. But eventually she could wait no longer.

> *I could see the gap in the fence and I made a run for it. I traded in the Kurt Geiger shoes and the Alfa Romeo for a pair of trainers and a sturdy custom-built Condor cycle.*

Off she went, travelling west to east along ancient trade routes and paths trod by pilgrims. Roman roads took her through Europe, while from Greece to the ancient Indus Valley in South Asia she followed in Alexander the Great's footsteps. Through Pakistan and India she travelled the Imperial Road with the Moghuls, and across the USA the mail delivery route of the Pony Express was her guide. The road presented many challenges, but humour and optimism were her tactics for dealing with the problems that arose. Unaccompanied woman travellers are unusual, in those days more so, and she attracted much attention; unwanted advances and crowds of curious children were robustly dealt with by channelling her past personality of Head Teacher.

Over a period of 15 months she travelled 12,000 miles and returned 23 lb lighter, with a passion for cycling, writing and travelling. Tales of her adventures, and the places and people that she encountered, were collected in the book *A Bike Ride: 12,000 miles around the world*. Keen for others to experience this wonderful new life, she wrote another, with advice for those setting out on a long-distance tour for the first time.

Five years later she set out again on another circumnavigation, this time east to west, following the route of the Spanish and Portuguese colonisers – the Conquistadors – across South America, before sailing as Captain Cook across the Pacific. The Silk Road would lead her from China back to Europe.

Anne had found a new and unexpected career as a travel writer at an age when most would be concentrating on their retirement. Her writing gained acclaim and she became sought after as a lecturer.

Her newfound career was to last until the end of her life. In 2009, after 22 years and over 100,000 miles of touring, she set off on another ultra long-distance trip, which, tragically, was to be her last. After just a couple of months on the road she fell ill in Aleppo, Syria, and died, aged 76.

To others who might follow in her footsteps she has shown that one need not be young and fit or have any prior knowledge of cycling in order to take on the ultimate adventure. Praised as an 'unlikely cyclist', 'her own woman' and 'a force of nature', she is credited as an inspiration by many.

Kyle Dempster – The road from Karakol

Two roads diverged, and I took the one less travelled.

On 22 August 2016 Kyle Dempster went missing from Pakistan's Ogre II along with climbing partner Scott Adamson. They were last seen partway up the north face the day before a storm engulfed the area. It was five days before the snow and cloud could clear enough for helicopters to make an aerial search, but there was no trace of the climbers. A week later the search was called off.

It was a tragic end to a life that had been stuffed to the brim with adventuring, usually involving snow, peaks and mountaineering. Of some small consolation to his family was that he died doing what he truly loved.

Back in 2011, Kyle had set out on a different kind of expedition, something that would take him out of his comfort zone and show him the world from a different angle. Ordinarily, his trips would involve landing in a mountain range and setting up base camp with a climbing partner, spending a few days scaling the peaks and then taking a boozy flight home. But on this occasion Kyle chose a bicycle instead of a partner, and the road over a base camp. This would be a climbing adventure on two wheels, traversing Kyrgyzstan from Karakol in the east, following the network of old Soviet roads westwards while scaling as many peaks as possible. He knew only a handful of Russian words and carried minimal climbing gear; he'd bought his bicycle a few weeks before leaving and had never previously cycle toured.

It was at once the most difficult adventure he'd attempted and the most wonderful. His bike was heavy and progress slow, up endless mountain drags, but his saddle was an incredible perch, 'as lofty as any summit from which to see this strange and wonderful place'. At times the eternal downhills would feel as if he were riding off the edge of the world.

He met locals and drank vodka with them; he was given food, drink and company, and began to get under the skin of the country that he would otherwise merely gaze down upon. At times he would ride for days with no sign of life other than distant herds of sheep. On barely paved roads, he found himself in the centre of mountain ranges that defied belief. Travelling alone, the bindings of modern society finally gave way.

> " *You no longer know where you end and where the world begins.*

After 19 days he'd pedalled almost 500 km. The road ahead began to dissolve, towns lying abandoned, the hollow shells of hotels, mines and homes standing empty after the collapse of the Soviet Union. Every so often he would pass a family carving a living from the hills. Nature had begun to reclaim the detritus of past habitation. 'Yet the road keeps going, a shortcut through an otherwise blank section of map.'

The broken tarmac stretched ahead, desert on either side, mountains in the distance capped with snow. To reach them seemed impossible, his wheels bucking over the rough surface, the road eventually morphing into a dirt track, then a sandy suggestion of a line and then nothing. Ahead, a river – no road other than the steep rocky banks. Sometimes able to ride, sometimes able to do nothing more than carry his bike and trailer over water-lapped rocks, he made slow and painful progress. The river was too deep to ford. There was nothing to be done but to follow the river and see where it led.

After 40 days of travelling an average of a mere 20 km per day, the inevitable became reality: the river would have to be crossed. The appearance of a bridge was becoming more improbable with every passing kilometre. Anchoring one of his ropes to a rock, he waded into the water, the flow fast, the bed deep, every sense on crystal-sharp alert as his experience of high-adrenaline challenges was put to the test. Fully aware of the potential for disaster, he filmed a moving goodbye to his family in case he didn't make it – a video which is hugely poignant now.

But he did make it safely to the opposite bank where, for the first time in two weeks, a paved road stretched ahead. The test was over. He zoomed along infinite descents, scattering sheep in all directions. And there, ahead, were the peaks he'd been seeking, covered in snow. He left his bike and scaled the slopes, on top of the world.

'Real adventure isn't polished. There's no hashtag for it. It exists at the intersection of the imagination and the ridiculous. It will find you there. And when it does, remember, there's just one question. In this life, when the road comes to an end, will you keep pedalling?'

Scott Stoll – The ultimate adventure

*A bicycle ride around the world begins
with a single pedal stroke.*

It is a true test of one's bravery and resolve to set out on a journey that could easily end in failure. To undertake a challenge that seems so impossibly vast can make it almost inconceivable to even set the first pedal in motion. Fear of the unknown can be crippling; comfort is found in the safe, easy, life – a life that can become static, mundane and eat away at your spirit.

Scott Stoll's experience of that life reached its critical point when he lost his job, his girlfriend and best friend. 'I felt that I was running a maze like a mouse being told that some imaginary chunk of cheese was in my future if I did just the right thing and followed just the right path.' He lost his faith, both in God and in himself. The answers he sought wouldn't come from bosses, books, preachers or teachers. 'If life had a meaning, the answer had to be out there somewhere. I vowed to find happiness or die trying.'

For Scott, the answer would come only with the ultimate adventure: a bike ride around the globe. His 'warm-up' ride across the USA revealed more than ever that he wouldn't be an educated person until he had seen the world.

So on 6 September 2001, Scott pedalled away from his home in San Francisco, filled in equal measure with trepidation and excitement. Ahead was the unknown, a path that had so far existed only in his imagination and on the scribbled maps hung around his bedroom walls.

Five days after leaving, terrorists flew two aeroplanes into the towers of the World Trade Center in New York. The attacks changed everything; confused and frightened, Scott wondered if he should continue. The world was no longer the same. There might be people out there who would hate him just for being American. It took some serious deliberation to realise that shutting himself away from the rest of the world wasn't the answer; now more than ever was the time to embrace different cultures, to get to know people, to find out what motivated them, and to encourage unity rather than division. So Scott labelled himself the Bicycling Ambassador, an American citizen who, despite the political upheaval and rhetoric, would head out into the world with an open mind and an open heart.

From San Francisco he rode south to Argentina, then across Europe, into India and towards China. Tackling the unforgiving trail to Mount Everest Base Camp, he fell into conversation with a group of climbers preparing to begin their ascent. 'What you're doing is amazing – we could never do that,' they told him. 'Likewise,' Scott replied, and they all laughed, realising that 'impossible' is just a state of mind.

Through the magic of bicycle travel, countries and cultures morphed imperceptibly into the next and as he made his way across the continents, Scott began to experience the spirituality he had sought; a natural ebb and flow had replaced the clockwork nature of his previous life. The world was a beautiful canvas upon which he could draw whatever he chose. 'I am a painter and the brush is my bicycle.'

After China he cycled through Southeast Asia and the silver beaches of Thailand, through the vast outback of Australia and the sacred lands of the Aborigines, then through New Zealand, home to the kiwi bird and the land of rainbows. The world tour was completed with a 6,500-mile African safari. It took four years to complete his travels, years during which his experiences had ranged from pure survival to pure enlightenment. After 31,500 miles of riding he arrived home, a new man.

Returning to a post-9/11 America was a major difficulty. Nobody truly understood what he had experienced or learned. It would take time to apply the lessons of the road to a life of stasis in a world in turmoil – turmoil from which, for four years, he'd been immune. For after the ultimate adventure, what comes next?

But despite these questions, Scott's fundamental discovery had been that we humans have more in common than we realise, with the same kinds of doubts, fears, hopes and dreams. Everyone, dozens of times a day, would ask the same questions: How are you? Where are you going? What are you doing? Where do you sleep? Do you miss your family? Are you happy? To that last question, he could finally answer, 'Yes.'

'I began my trip feeling afraid and lost, but I didn't know that the very best adventure is unimaginable and impossible until it is done. Humans instinctively fear the unknown. Life is not easy. But you can create yourself to be a hero; if you have the passion and the courage, you will find the way.'

Billie Fleming – The Rudge-Whitworth Keep Fit Girl

When the spirits are low, when the day appears dark, when work becomes monotonous, when hope hardly seems worth having, just mount a bicycle and go out for a spin down the road, without thought on anything but the ride you are taking.
ARTHUR CONAN DOYLE

In 1911, a competition was promoted by *Cycling* magazine for the highest number of 'centuries' (100 miles) ridden in a single year. Said to be inspired by Harry Long, a commercial traveller who, in the course of his work, had ridden 25,000 miles through England and Scotland in one year, the competition soon evolved into a challenge for the highest total mileage recorded over a 12-month period. Many riders took up the challenge, but it wasn't until 1938 that a woman attempted it.

Billie Fleming had been taught to ride a bicycle at the age of 18 and had become instantly besotted. To her, the bicycle meant freedom, with fitness as an added bonus. The concept of exercise as a worthy leisure pursuit was emerging at that time; the Women's League of Health and Beauty held group fitness sessions to encourage women to get out of the home and do something active. Billie wholeheartedly agreed – though she would far rather go out for a bike ride than go to an exercise class.

A competition for bike riding seemed the natural thing to do, given that Billie already rode her bike every day. By taking part she could promote cycling as a means of fitness to other women. The bike manufacturer Rudge-Whitworth agreed to donate a bicycle, and Cadbury's pledged to send her 5 lb of chocolate every month. Her decision raised more than a few eyebrows but she was undaunted: 'I was young and fit and ready to take on anything.'

On 1 January 1938, the 'Rudge-Whitworth Keep Fit Girl' set off from central London and cycled the 70 miles to Aylesbury in Buckinghamshire and back to her home in Mill Hill, Hertfordshire. Every day that followed, whatever the weather, she would wake, pack her modest belongings in her saddle bag and go for a ride. Her simple three-speed bicycle became her best friend. She travelled light, with just a change of clothes and a few tools, relying on cafes and passing help for food and water – she carried not even a water bottle. Through the short winter days she explored the countryside surrounding London before returning home each night, and as spring approached she began to venture further afield, taking lodgings in B & Bs as she pedalled throughout England.

By late spring, Billie had become quite the celebrity, her journeys attracting much reporting in the media. She used her fame to extol the benefits of cycling, writing articles for *Cycling* magazine which appealed for '1,000,000 more women cyclists,' and in the evenings giving talks at the village hall or bike shop. Though mostly riding alone, she would be joined on occasion by her husband, or by the cycling clubs in the areas through which she passed. Newspapers spoke of her relentless energy and determination which were always accompanied by a smile.

Into a balmy summer she rode, pedalling around the north of England and Scotland, travelling as far north as Loch Lomond. Wherever she went, she would ask passers-by to sign witness cards as evidence of her mileage, which were then posted to *Cycling* magazine in order for them to ratify the record. Her plan each day was no more elaborate than seeing where her wheels would take her, exploring as much or as little as she felt. Waking in York one morning, she decided to cycle home, all 186 miles. That day's ride was the highlight of the year.

Maintaining an average of 81 miles a day, she continued into a bitter winter, steadily accruing a total of 29,600 miles. Her love of riding never waned, even on those days when the rain threatened and the snow fell, when she rose in candlelight and could see her breath on the cold morning air. 'You have to really want to do it,' she said.

> *Whatever the weather is that morning, you have to put your clothes on and get on and ride the bike. You will have bad days, but the good days make up for all of the bad ones.*

Billie continued riding throughout her life, the legacy of 'The Rudge-Whitworth Keep Fit Girl' encouraging women through the decades to take to two wheels. In 2015 the Tribute to Billie ride saw women from all over the UK ride each day, roughly following her mileage and her routes, taking up Billie's mantle in her quest for a million more women riders.

And Billie was right: all that cycling was good for her. She lived to the age of 100.

Tommy Godwin – Marathon man

Nothing compares to the simple pleasure of a bike ride.
JOHN F. KENNEDY

The first official winner of the *Cycling* magazine competition for most miles ridden in a year was Frenchman Marcel Plaines who rode 34,000 miles in 1911. His record stood for 20 years before another attempt was made: in the 1930s, eight cyclists from Great Britain, France and Australia each tried to beat it.

In 1939 Tommy Godwin, a keen cyclist and local time trial champion, decided to have a go. He would be going head to head with two other Englishmen: Edward Swann and Bernard Bennett.

The marketing potential of such challenges was huge – in an age when companies would compete to demonstrate that their bicycles were the most reliable, what better way to prove so than to have it ridden every single day for a year?

Initially sponsored by Ley Cycles, Godwin set off into a snowy January. On ice-covered roads and with limited daylight hours, he crashed several times and was hospitalised twice in the first two months. Poor road surfaces and a heavy bicycle did nothing to aid his efforts. But onwards he strove, heading down to the West Country where the weather was better, easily taking the lead over his two rivals despite his tribulations.

By spring, Swann had withdrawn, Ley Cycles had gone out of business and Bennett had begun to claw back the lead. Godwin's sponsorship was taken on by Raleigh, and, as the weather improved, both riders blasted into the summer months, urged by their pacers and sponsors to post ever higher daily mileages. The luxury of sleep was reduced to 40 hours a week; cycling would begin at 5 a.m., with 50 miles pedalled before breakfast. The riders would sleep in fields or collapse exhausted onto friends' sofas, unable to remove their own sodden woollens. In July alone Godwin rode 8,583 miles. Things were getting out of hand so a mutual agreement to scale things back was made.

The outbreak of war in September brought rationing and blackouts; headlights required taping, and Godwin's vegetarian diet of cheese, bread, milk and eggs was further restricted. After a sustained effort of 200+ mile days, Godwin passed the record in late October, a month ahead of Bennett.

But he didn't stop riding; he kept going to the end of the year, by which time he had ridden 75,065 miles. Still he persisted, pedalling into the following spring to clock up 100,000 miles in 500 days. Finally able to stop, but unable to uncurl his hands, he spent the next few months learning to walk again.

Godwin was elevated to the status of a celebrity. Subsequent attempts were discouraged – it was deemed too dangerous.

Then in 2015, after the UltraMarathon Cycling Association agreed to ratify any future records, two men took on the historic challenge: British Steven Abraham and American Kurt 'Tarzan' Searvogel. Abraham set out on a Raleigh steel-framed bicycle, as Godwin had done, hoping to follow similar routes, but a collision with a moped after three months left him with a broken ankle and he eventually withdrew. As the year drew to a close, Searvogel passed the record, and five days later he'd added another thousand miles, reaching 76,076 miles – a tribute to the incredible Godwin, whose record had stood for 76 years.

CHAPTER SIX
THE NEED FOR SPEED

Guy Martin – Britain's fastest cyclist

I want to go as fast as humanly possible, on whatever it is... I just love going fast.

For a long time humans have been obsessed with speed. Creating, innovating, pushing boundaries, increasing efficiency, going harder, stronger and faster than anyone before. Ever since the bicycle was invented, people have wanted to race. As technology has progressed, so has our concept of speed. The first land speed record was set in the early twentieth century and since then it has been bettered again and again. With jet boosters and rockets, speeds of over 1,000 kph have been reached. But how fast is it possible to go with human power alone? How fast can a bicycle go?

Guy Martin is a self-professed speed freak. A motorcycle racer, he's familiar with zooming around a time trial track at an average speed of 200 mph. He is the fastest ever rider on the motorcycle Wall of Death: a gravity-defying stunt that sees riders circling the inside of a cylinder, held in place by centrifugal force and experiencing stresses of up to 8G. He's always loved bicycles, from the BMX he would practise stunts on as a child, to the push bike on which he'd do his paper round and the road bike he now rides to work. Merging one passion with another, in late 2013 Guy set out to achieve the British land speed record for a bicycle.

The existing record stood at 110 mph, set in 1986 by professional racer Dave Le Grys, who drafted a modified racing car on the unopened M42. 'It scared the life out of me,' he said. 'You gotta be kind of nuts to do it.'

Drafting, or slipstreaming, has helped cyclists to increase their speed for over 100 years, from the early cycle racers who would ride behind tandems or motorised dernies to Charles 'Mile-a-Minute' Murphy who, at the turn of the nineteenth century, drafted a train to achieve a speed of 60 mph, becoming the first man to ever cycle a mile in under a minute. But drafting a vehicle at speed is dangerous — mistakes can be fatal. If at any point the rider were to exit the slipstream, it would be like hitting a solid wall of air. In 1952, Frenchman José Meiffret's record attempt ended in near tragedy when his tyres exploded at 80 mph and he tumbled for 300 ft, fracturing his skull in five places.

Realistic about the risks, and with a flash of his trademark boyish grin, Guy summed up the challenge:

> It's going to be tough. I like a bit of danger. I haven't got a death wish but it makes things exciting. If it

was easy every man and his dog would be doing it.

After months of training and preparation, Guy was ready. The bicycle had been specially made by renowned frame builders Rourke, with a frame capable of maintaining stability at triple-figure speeds and a compound gearing system: with two 60-tooth chain rings rigged in sequence, for every rotation of the pedals the wheel would turn 15 times. Guy would be riding behind a 5.5 ton racing lorry, with the British truck racing champion at the wheel. He had been coached by Olympic track cyclist Laura Trott and had been working hard on his fitness.

The attempt was to take place at Pendine Sands, a 7-mile sweep of beach in South Wales. Common as a location for setting records, it was where racing motorist Malcolm Campbell had broken the motor land speed record numerous times in the 1920s and 1930s, reaching 146 mph in his Bluebird. A tow line would bring Guy's pace up to 60 mph – gears designed for these kinds of speeds are difficult to turn from a standing start.

Even as the tow line was released, Guy was in trouble: sand kicked up from the huge truck wheels meant that a virtual sandstorm was billowing around him, the grains finding their way into his visor. All he could focus on was the huge white board that had been mounted on the back of the truck to act as a spoiler, increasing the area of slipstream in which he could ride. At such a terrific pace, the gentle curve of the beach was magnified, making it almost impossible to steer. But with an incredible effort and nerves of steel, he sustained a speed of over 100 mph for a mile, shaking from head to toe with adrenaline as he came to a stop. 'I think that's the maddest thing I've ever seen on a bike,' declared one of his teammates. And Guy had done what he'd set out to do: he had ridden his bicycle at 112.94 mph to become Britain's fastest cyclist.

Tom Donhou – The 100-mile-an-hour bike

It started out as just an idea – to simply build a bike and see how fast we could go.

Tom Donhou, a frame builder from East London, spent a lot of time in his workshop wondering about the potential of the machines he was making. He'd always been interested in the land speed record attempts, fascinated by the enthusiasts in the 1960s who had built cars in their sheds and then taken them out on the salt flats. It was the haphazard nature of it all that attracted him – piecing something together, relying solely on your own skill and the materials to hand. Scottish racer Graeme Obree had once pedalled into the record books on a bike he'd built himself using a bundle of old BMX tubes and a bottom bracket famously constructed with bearings from an old washing machine.

The world record for speed on a bicycle is held by Dutchman Fred Rompelberg who, in 1995, rode across the Bonneville Salt Flats in the US state of Utah in the slipstream of a dragster. He reached a top speed of 167 mph. In 2016, a new women's record was set in the same location by Californian Denise Mueller, who reached 147 mph.

The conditions of this record attempt would be very different from Fred Rompelberg's. Salt flats are fast, flat and empty in every direction. Tom's first attempt would be on a dual carriageway. Dragsters can reach top speeds of 335 mph. Tom would be using his old car, a 1950s Ford Zephyr, with a top speed of... Well, they were yet to find out.

Tom built the bike in his own workshop, using components that he would normally use for his customers: this was to look and feel as much like a regular bike as possible. It had a simple but strong frame, with handlebars dropped extra low to keep his profile in the Zephyr's slipstream. With a 104-tooth chain ring – over twice the size of what you'd find on a regular bicycle – he would be able to cruise at 70 mph and hopefully push it to more than 100 mph. A plywood spoiler was added to the rear of the car to increase the slipstream.

The day of the test run arrived. They headed out early while traffic was light, with Tom riding a nerve-testing 6 inches off the back of the car; no tow line, no buffer-bar to prevent crashing – just a two-way radio so driver and rider could communicate. The speed increased steadily, until they reached 60 mph; Gav, driving the Zephyr, was not used to the column-shift gear system and skipped a gear, causing a sudden jolt which nearly catapulted Tom from his bike. It was fraught, and as the traffic began to build up, they decided to leave it at that. Without closed roads it was the best they could do.

The attempt itself was made in early 2013 on an old disused airstrip. They swept and prepared the track, and marked out the line. The nerves began to kick in.

The first few attempts didn't quite work. Gav was pulling away too fast and couldn't hear Tom trying to tell him so through the helmet microphone. If the car went too quickly,

Tom would lose the slipstream and be unable to keep up. The acceleration had to be smooth and at a specific rate – once the gear starts turning, it doesn't want to stop. With only 2 miles in which to coordinate everything before the air strip ended, the day was becoming frustrating.

Then, on one attempt, everything fell into place. 'Go, go, go!' Tom was screaming, feeling the big cog turning, propelling him forward, as the car dragged him along behind. The speedo crept up to 80 mph. Gav's foot was to the floor; they had reached top speed.

Tom said:

> *The feeling was incredible. We'd gone as fast as the car could go, and we'd run out of road. That's all we could hope for.*

Later, Tom set the bike up on rollers and pedalled his way past 100 mph. Perhaps in the future they might try again with a faster car.

'In the end it wasn't about setting records. It was about using our imagination, being resourceful. It was an exercise in bicycle design, backyard aerodynamics, and the pioneering spirit of using what you've got and doing the best you can.'

Sir Bradley Wiggins – The Hour record

> *The Hour is one of the hardest challenges a cyclist can take on.*
> JACK BOBRIDGE

Way back in 1873, James Moore decided to see how far he could cycle in an hour. He rode his penny-farthing a distance of 23 km. It was an unofficial record, but it started an obsession that would last down the years: who can ride the furthest in an hour?

It's as pure as it is difficult – no one to chase, no tactics, no pacing your opponents before dropping them – a straightforward test of speed: rider vs clock, competing on a level playing field across time and space.

The allure of the Hour draws cyclists from every walk of life, amateurs and professionals alike. Pretty much every cycling great has had a crack at the Hour: Coppi's 1942 record of 45.8 km stood for 14 years before Anquetil broke it; then it was over to Merckx, who took the title in 1972 with a distance of 49.4 km. He declared it to be: 'The hardest ride I have ever done.' By the time Induráin made an attempt, the parameters had changed: in an effort to go ever faster, bicycle design was being pushed to the limit, with disc wheels, aero bars, carbon frames and unconventional styles of riding proliferating. Graeme Obree's record saw him crouched low in a 'skier's tuck'; Chris Boardman pioneered the 'superman' pose on super-extended racing bars. The UCI decreed that only efforts using equipment akin to what Merckx would have used would be deemed Hour records; all other attempts would be classed as Best Human Effort.

In 2014, the rules were again revised: the UCI brought the guidance for Hour records in line with track racing, relaxing the strict ruling on equipment, and set the mark to beat at 49.7 km: Czech Ondrej Sosenka's 2005 record. There followed a flurry of attempts. Jens Voigt of Germany was the first who, in September 2014 at the age of 43, smashed the record with a distance of 51.115 km. It stood for a mere six weeks: in October, Austrian rider Matthias Brändle took the title with a distance of 51.853 km. Three months later Australian Jack Bobridge had a go but couldn't quite top the record, so fellow countryman Rohan Dennis was the next to triumph, in February 2015, with a distance of 52.491 km. The Dutchman Thomas Dekker and Swede Gustav Larsson made their attempts in February and March respectively, both unable to beat Dennis. In May it was Alex Dowsett's turn and the Brit triumphed with a distance of 52.937 km. Five weeks later, Bradley Wiggins stepped up to the plate at London's VeloPark.

Wiggins had been racing on the international stage since 2000 and came to the attention of British audiences in 2012, when he won the Tour de France – the first Brit ever to do so. That turned out to be his year: after striking the gong at the opening ceremony of the London Olympics, he went on to win gold in the individual time trial, adding to his three existing Olympic gold medals – a total that would reach five in Rio. He won BBC Sports Personality of the Year and ended 2012 with a knighthood. Affectionately known as Wiggo, the Modfather of British cycling, after the 2012 Tour he also earned himself the nickname Le Gentleman, when he slowed the peloton to enable it to regroup after saboteurs had thrown tacks on the road.

On 7 June 2015, the Lee Valley VeloPark was at capacity, the home crowd the perfect backdrop to Wiggins' record attempt. The venue held huge significance for Wiggins, having been built on the site of the Eastway cycle track on which he'd raced as a Junior. Impatient to be on his way, he began a few minutes ahead of the scheduled time, with the roars of an excited crowd fading into the background as he settled to his task. It was just him and the track, a red line to follow round and round until either the clock won or he did.

From the outset it was clear that Wiggins was going to pull off an extraordinary performance. Screens around the venue showed, with each lap, how far ahead of the record he was. His gold aerodynamic helmet, tapering to a point, sat perfectly level with his flat back. The bike he rode was as modified as possible without breaking the rules. Steadily increasing his speed, his lead on Dowsett's record grew as he rode that endless circle. With no water, in a packed velodrome that had been heated to 28°C to create the optimum conditions for the attempt, Wiggins grew red in the face as the hour ticked by, but his pace simply escalated. The challenge is the timing: peak too soon and you'll be running on empty, but equally you don't want to reach the end with anything left in the tank. It would have taken months of training and preparation for this, and he timed it to perfection: as he built towards the final few laps, the crowd were on their feet, going wild for this extraordinary cyclist, urging him towards his finish line and a place in the record books.

As the bell chimed for the hour, Wiggins completed his 218th lap having ridden a distance of 54.526 km. Miguel Induráin was among the crowd and came to congratulate him, and to welcome him to the exclusive list of riders who have set the Hour record and also won the Tour de France.

Wiggins retired the following year. Asked where the Hour record ranked in his extensive list of achievements, Wiggins commented: 'I had such great memories here as a kid and to come here as an old man… it tops it off.'

Mike Hall – Fastest man around the world

It wasn't cycling round the world like many would know it, but it was my kind of race.

Many people have cycled the world and many have ended up in the record books as the fastest. But in 2012, circling the planet became an official race: the World Cycle Race. When Mike Hall from Yorkshire wheeled up to the start line in Greenwich on 18 February 2012, a passer-by said to him, 'You look like you're going to be time trialling round the world!'

'I am,' Mike replied.

The rules of the race are to ride a minimum of 18,000 miles in an easterly or westerly direction, starting and ending in the same place and passing through two antipodal points en route. Total distance travelled, including transits across oceans, should be at least 25,000 miles (the length of the Equator). Competitors should aim to complete their ride in the quickest possible time. For in spite of the distance, this is definitely racing, not touring. Bikes are exceptionally light; packing is for survival. Panniers are shunned in favour of frame bags. A down jacket might be used instead of a sleeping bag. A bivvy suffices to keep the rain out.

Mike's previous experience in endurance racing had been in the Tour Divide, a 2,745 mile mountain-biking race along the spine of the Rocky Mountains from Canada to Mexico: an unsupported, single-stage event where competitors must carry all they need and the clock never stops. The lessons he learned about fuelling on the move, packing light and sleeping little were applied to the World Cycle Race – it would be essentially the same, but on a road bike and much, much longer.

In a bag no larger than a small knapsack, he carried a tent with an inflatable pole, sleeping bag, jacket and sleeping mat, waterproof trousers and a gilet. A change of clothes would have been an extravagance. The kit was strapped beneath the saddle and in the triangle of the frame, in line with his body in order to minimise any drag factor. His bicycle was made of carbon fibre. The whole thing weighed less than 18 kg.

> *I didn't need to take equipment, I just needed to take risks.*

And Mike certainly took risks. 'The winner will be the one who lives fast, not necessarily the one who rides fast,' he said. His average mileage was 200 miles a day, with a century ridden before lunch and another squeezed in before bed. On most days he was still riding at 10 p.m., pushing on until he was almost falling from his bike with tiredness; sleep was snatched in bushes, at roadsides, on beaches, beneath bus shelters and in public toilets.

Initially, the biggest challenge was the physicality of all that riding: the strain, the fatigue, the sleep deprivation. As time went on, the mental side became tougher: unfamiliar terrains, alien cultures and the sheer length of the task. In other races, you can just tough it out but in this it was endless: 'After a couple of weeks you can't remember when you started and you can't imagine the end.'

Despite the gruelling nature of the challenge, Mike never lacked the motivation to get up and grind out another 200 miles. Even when the weather was bad or enthusiasm was lacking, he knew it would be just as punishing for the other nine competitors.

> *You've always got to tell yourself, when you're going through a bad patch – this won't last. And when you're going through a good patch, that won't last either.*

Mike rolled into Greenwich after 107 days. He had spent 91 days on his bicycle and ridden 18,175 miles, finishing 5,000 miles ahead of his closest challenger and coming in two weeks faster than the previous record holder. To top it off, his victory was achieved on the day he turned 31.

The experience cemented Mike's enthusiasm for endurance racing. In 2013 he entered the Tour Divide again, and won. The following year he won the inaugural Trans America Bike Race – a gruelling 4,400 miles from the Pacific coast to the Atlantic, with no support vehicles, no teams and no prize money – the antithesis to the fully supported and long-running Race Across America (RAAM).

His passion for adventure racing led to him founding, in 2013, the Transcontinental Race, an event he describes as beautifully simple yet completely ridiculous. Competitors travel across continental Europe from west to east via the Alps, solo and unsupported, with only the start point, finish point and a few check points dictated – the rest is up to the riders. Racing on this scale is growing in popularity: although only 30 people registered for the first edition of the race, over 1,000 people applied in 2016.

One might suppose that it's vital to be very single-minded to achieve such feats, but Mike's a chaotic chap, always half-finishing things: cups of tea half drunk, pencils put down in odd places. Not that this is a problem, because when you're on the bike, it's all about riding. 'My mind is kind of racing along. I don't care what it does. That's one of the things I love: all the time, you're still riding a bike.'

Juliana Buhring – The healing power of two wheels

Out of the hottest fire comes the strongest steel.
CHINESE PROVERB

Juliana's is a tale of an extraordinary woman who, overcome by grief when her partner was killed on a kayaking expedition, set off on a bike ride around the world. She couldn't see a way through the pain of losing him: 'I was too cowardly to kill myself, but I thought the trip might do it for me.' It was a remarkable feat to undertake, not least because the last time she had ridden a bicycle she was a child – and that had had training wheels. 'Nobody believed I would make it, certainly not all the way around the world.'

But a drastic decision was something that she needed to take. Her grief ran deeper than just her loss, back to a childhood spent in the clutches of the infamous Christian fundamentalist cult, Children of God. Subjected to beatings, enforced silence and sleep deprivation, she was separated from her mother at the age of four and lived in 30 different countries, managing to get out at the age of 23. Life started again, with nothing. Juliana's anger turned to resilience – the kind of resilience that would keep the pedals turning all the way around the world.

> *I was not an athlete and not a cyclist. In fact, there was nothing to qualify me for such a huge undertaking. Nothing but willpower and the determination to finish, no matter what. I was out to prove anything is possible.*

With no commercial backers and very little money, after just eight months of training, Juliana set off to chase a record that no one had set before: to become the fastest woman to cycle around the world. She could have continued her preparation, but she might never have left. 'Many people postpone making their dreams a reality to wait for the perfect time. There is no such thing. The perfect time is right now.'

Never having had a settled home and always having relied on herself, Juliana found that her steely independence, adaptability and capacity to cope with the physical struggles of the ride meant that life on the road came naturally. 'I have a really high tolerance for pain, and I feel the need to just push through where a lot of people would have finished a long time ago.'

But despite thriving on solitude, it was the discovery of the kindness of strangers that became so formative to Juliana: caught out in the New Zealand mountains with a wind so strong it picked up her bicycle, suffering the onset of hypothermia, with the nearest town miles away, she knocked on the door of a camper and was invited inside for whisky and sausages.

Through the freedom of the open road, Juliana was able to find what she'd been looking for. 'I had been such a stunted child in a tiny world; I just wanted to make up for all of that lost time.' The simplicity of travelling, of having no greater task than to ride, brought such peace that she began to heal. It took a few months for her to finally find closure. 'In the middle of the Nullarbor desert in Australia, I knew that life had to move on. It was as much of an emotional moving on as it was physical.'

She returned – 144 days pedalled, 152 days travelled, a total of 29,060 km crossing 19 countries and 4 continents, averaging 200 km per day – to become the fastest woman in the world. And there began a love affair with long-distance racing that would give her a name as one of the world's fastest ultra-endurance cyclists.

She raced the Transcontinental in 2013, the only woman to do so, and came ninth out of 31 riders, cycling 3,600 km in 12 days and 2 hours. The following year it was the inaugural Trans America Bike Race, which she completed in 20 days and 23 hours, despite suffering a cracked rib and a pinched nerve, to become the first woman and fourth overall, after a 36-hour sprint for the finish line.

'I set off around the world to exorcise the pain, to save myself. I had no idea where it would lead.'

Lael Wilcox – Defying her detractors

For me, the racing is fun but the riding is much more important.

Lael Wilcox lives on a bike. No fixed place to call home, she wanders the land with her boyfriend, more often sleeping outside than indoors, always looking for the next adventure. An experienced bike-packer, she's never happier than when on two wheels. Not what many would class a typical cyclist, with no Lycra and no padded cycling shorts, she often rides in running shoes. Though more at home on a mountain bike, long-distance road racing slipped naturally into her life, and in 2016 she entered the Trans America Bike Race.

Following the TransAmerica Bicycle Trail for 4,400 miles from Astoria, Oregon on the Pacific coast, to Yorktown, Virginia on the Atlantic coast, it's a route ridden by thousands of touring cyclists each year. But like any endurance race, the target is time: anything longer than 40 days and it stops looking like a race. It's tough, mentally and physically, with brutal mountain climbs and vast open plains where sun-scorched vegetation withers in 40°C heat. There are sections where the nearest shop is a day's ride away. The race is unsupported – riders must carry all they need. It's an event that pushes the limits of endurance to the next level, a level in which even professionals don't compete. As 2014 women's winner Juliana Buhring put it: 'This is just for the crazies.'

As a warm-up, Lael rode to the start line from Anchorage, Alaska – 1,000 miles across Canada to Oregon before she'd even begun. Anticipating warm weather for at least the first few days, she sent her sleeping bag home – it was a luxury she could do without.

The battle is with the other competitors, with the road and with nature. Fighting traffic, it's often safer to ride on the highway's hard shoulder, though the surface is unsurfaced, rough and gravelly, slippery in the rain and dusty in the sun. The route traverses bear territory, meaning that bivvying on the mountainside involves little sleep. In the stifling heat riding becomes unbearable. Desperate for respite Lael would jump into any streams, rivers and lakes she could find, fully clothed – including her shoes. Rain howls and skies are ripped with lightning, forks of electricity striking the ground. In the vast plains of the Midwest, there is no shelter.

In its difficulty lies its attraction: the self-sufficient survival, the thrill of the race, the empowerment inherent in riding a bike for multiple thousands of miles, the astounding landscapes, the brushes with wildlife, the sunsets, the drivers who pull over to offer you a bottle of water. The publicity says:

> *If you have a wild itch to cycle day and night, then perhaps this is for you.*

Lael put in an extraordinary performance. Averaging 237 miles per day, resting for just 3–5 hours per night and eating meals on the bike, she was in the top three from the start and the leading woman throughout. As has historically been the case, it's never expected that a woman might win an event such as this. That's the preserve of the men: strong, tough guys who would naturally occupy the first few spots.

The race leader, Greek rider Steffen Streich, was in Lael's sights. Not since the start line had she seen him, in the midst of nervous anticipation and tentative well wishes, though that memory had long since faded. He was within touching distance – she knew she could win this race. She scaled back sleep in the last two nights and gained ground.

When going to sleep, it's customary for competitors to leave their bicycle facing the direction of travel, as on long, nondescript roads, waking from brief, mind-numbing naps, it's easy to mistake which way to go. Perhaps Steffen had placed his bike incorrectly, perhaps he had awoken disorientated or perhaps he'd been confused in the dark, but on the last night of the ride, he set off on his sprint to the finish line in the wrong direction, not realising his mistake until he saw a bright light coming towards him. It was Lael. He rode past and then looped back, joining her, riding side by side. 'What's your name?' she asked. 'Steffen.' She immediately broke away and Steffen gave chase, the pair locked in a dead sprint for an incredible 25 miles. In her haste Lael took a wrong turn; Steffen called out to her, correcting her error, then venturing, 'You know, we've been pacing each other for so long, how about we just finish this thing together?' Lael looked sideways at him. 'Yeah right – this is a race!' and off she went. Steffen never caught her.

She crossed the finishing line two hours ahead of her rival, becoming the first woman ever to win the race, and beating Juliana Buhring's record by nearly three days.

There are always people who will make negative comments about an adventurer's achievements, spreading disbelieving or disparaging remarks about how the person couldn't possibly have accomplished everything they did. In the aftermath of the race, Lael received abuse online, mainly from men, who questioned her legitimacy in winning. But it's not brute strength that's required for this type of racing: it's mental strength, your capacity to recover and push through the pain, and how you plan your strategy. As Juliana

Buhring says, 'Women have plenty of spare fat and burn it more efficiently, plus we have a pretty high pain tolerance mentally and physically.' Lael's answer to those who might slight her performance is simple: 'People are in their houses sitting behind their computers trying to take away from what I've done. We're not even engaging in the same world at that point.'

Laura Trott – Olympic superstar

The minute I sit on a bike I am a different person.

The first velodromes were built in the mid-to-late nineteenth century for one purpose: speed. Surfaces are smooth and low-friction; bicycles are lightweight and streamlined, with one fixed gear and no brakes; corners are banked at a sharp angle so bicycle and rider are perpendicular to the track as they lean into the turn. The velodrome is a place where records are constantly broken, speeds are constantly bettered and spectators flock to watch the dizzying performance of the fastest bicycle riders of the time.

The six-event omnium, Latin for 'of all', is a test of endurance, of tactics, but mostly of speed. Who can find the edge? Who can dig the deepest and discover that final burst to creep ahead? So often it comes down to fractions of wheel lengths. It begins with the scratch race, where riders battle it out in a 3,000 m sprint, followed by the individual pursuit: a pair of riders setting off at opposite sides of the track and chasing each other. Next is the elimination race, where every second lap sees the rider at the back of the field ruled out, and then the time trial, where riders complete four loops of the 250 m track against the clock. The flying lap follows, with riders building up their speed for one and a half laps before a 200 m timed sprint, and finally is the points race.

Laura Trott went into the points race at Rio 2016 with a 24-point lead accumulated from the previous five events. Her sprinting prowess is formidable, the ease with which she performs each discipline impressive. In the individual pursuit she caught her rival with 1 km to go and cruised to a win in the elimination race, finding time to wave to the crowd on the final straight. Her flying lap time set a new world record. She'd won all but one of the disciplines.

Off they went for the points race: 100 laps of the track with points awarded for the first riders to cross the line every tenth lap, and 20 points awarded to anyone who managed to lap the field. Round and round the velodrome they rode, like hamsters caught in the wheel, yet not once did the race succumb to monotony. Laura held off every one of her rivals who tried to inch up the table, and as the bell rang for the final lap, she took the outside path, overtaking Sarah Hammer of the USA and Belgian Jolien D'Hoore to sprint across the line in first place.

She had just pedalled her way into the record books: her gold medal in the omnium was added to the one she'd taken in the team sprint, making her the most successful British female Olympian of all time, with four gold medals in all.

With her height of just 5 feet 4 inches and slight build, she cuts a tiny figure on the track, but her litheness has made her one of the best cyclists of her generation. 'The best bike handler I've ever seen,' says Chris Hoy, while Victoria Pendleton has commented:

> *She might look fragile but it is the complete opposite of what is going on inside. She always pushes herself to the absolute limit.*

At the age of 12, Laura had met Bradley Wiggins, fresh from his gold medal triumph in Athens, who had hung his medal around her neck. Perhaps that was what had inspired a career that has so far seen her win 18 gold medals at world, European and Commonwealth level in addition to her four Olympic golds. She even won the British Road title in 2014, outsprinting Lizzie Armitstead.

Laura was born six weeks prematurely with a collapsed lung. She suffered asthma as a child. She was given her first bike aged four but she preferred trampolining, though she would frequently pass out in mid-air. She was advised to try cycling by the doctor, joining her older sister who was also a competitive cyclist, and her mother, who began cycling as a way to lose weight. A stomach condition sees her throwing up after a particularly tough training session or race. After the first event on the omnium she had her head in a bag.

'It just seems mad to me, honestly,' she says about her medal-winning performances. 'I just feel like that eight-year-old that started cycling because she absolutely loved it.'

CHAPTER SEVEN
CYCLING INNOVATORS

Jan Gehl – Making a city

Cycle lanes abound in Utopia.
H. G. WELLS

In a pavement cafe in a Copenhagen square sits a man with a glass of water and a notebook, watching people as they pass. As the seasons change, he continues to watch, pacing the city in shirtsleeves or huddling beneath an umbrella, identifiable by his wide-brimmed hat. A master of observation, he notes people's movements: the tracks they make from bus to building, and the manner in which they interact with man and object. Pages and pages are covered with diagrams and scrawl. This is Jan Gehl, urban planner.

Copenhagen is renowned as one of the most cycle-friendly cities in the world, but it wasn't always so. In the automobile boom of the 1960s, people abandoned their bicycles and began to drive. This miracle form of transport, so quick and easy, dry in all weathers, was a status symbol; to have one was to be rich. But then came the problems: congestion, ill health, laziness. The cycling fight-back was slow, stealthy and incremental – a protest against the dominance of the motor car, a gradual transformation of the streets that put the bicycle culture back at the forefront of city planning. Fierce resistance was encountered, but over a period of 40 years, Copenhagen became a cycling Utopia: a city admired by others around the world and a place where 45 per cent of commuters travel by bicycle. To 'Copenhagenize' is a recognised verb amongst cycle campaigners.

Gehl was among the people who worked on the Copenhagen revolution. With a degree in architecture, he married a psychologist who encouraged him to see the human side of buildings. Together they asked the question of why cities rarely appear to be built bearing in mind those who might use them. Historically, cities were formed around people: based on their needs, on a river or in the lee of the land, where the ground was rich or good for building. But over time, cities became overcrowded: their residents had less time, were unhappy and overweight, and developed respiratory diseases. For the majority of urban spaces, car was king. Planning seemed to focus on where to squeeze in more buildings rather than how to facilitate pedestrian movement. The answer to congestion was to build more roads.

Gehl's cities focussed on pedestrians and cyclists. Man is a walking animal after all – that's the speed at which our senses are engaged. It's not about being anti-car, just pro-people. What good was it to build cities that make traffic happy? Cars will fill whatever space you give them; it's how you use what's left that's important. So Gehl would watch, and make his notes, and learn from the most important users of cities: the people who lived there.

Change is not easy. There will always be resistance, especially if the benefits in the short term are not obvious. Initially, his beliefs were applauded but dismissed. His 1971 book, *Life Between Buildings*, was largely ignored. But Gehl knew he had something to say, something important. Inspiration came from Jane Jacobs, an American-Canadian urban activist who, in the 1960s, had shaken up planning practice by asking, 'Are we building cities for people or for cars?' It took a long time for Jacobs to be heard. 'Go out there and see what works,' she said. 'Look out of your windows, spend time in the streets and squares and see how people actually use spaces, and learn from that.'

So Gehl documented what he saw and used his observations to make changes that facilitated how people use space. Then he would analyse again, observe, make changes and repeat. There needn't be protest. 'If you do it slowly and don't tell anyone, no one will notice.'

In the 1990s Gehl was invited to work with the city of Melbourne to reduce its car culture. He recommended good cycling infrastructure, street cafes and outdoor seating, similar to the squares of Italy and France. He was ridiculed: 'It's too windy,' they said. 'The climate is too changeable. It will never work.' Yet Jan continued in his quiet way, watching, making changes and watching again. Melbourne now has the highest ratio of street furniture per person in the world and has been voted the most liveable city in the world six times.

Like Jane Jacobs, it has taken a long time for Gehl to be heard. His books, of which there are now many, are well-received; he is in demand worldwide by authorities that want to win back their cities from the motor car – cities hoping to 'do a Melbourne'. Even in the least likely places, where car culture seems to perpetuate, change is possible. Times Square in New York – for years a car park for the ubiquitous yellow taxi – underwent trial pedestrianisation in 2009, which has now been made permanent.

'It's about creating cities with a fundamental concern for life rather than the efficient flow of traffic. We can once again meet people, which is the reason people came to cities in the first place. A good city is like a good party. You know it's working when people stay for longer than necessary.'

Andrew Ritchie – Making a pocket-sized bike

I'm just a crazy guy who wanted to make the most human-friendly product that I could.

Barcelona, 2006: a group of men and women stand around in suits; they look ready for the office or perhaps for a drinks reception at a work do. Some wear neck ties, others flower-print dresses and silk gloves; there is an air of retro elegance and slight haphazardness to the collection. On closer inspection, they actually seem a bit odd. Despite the collared shirts and suit jackets, many of the gentlemen are wearing shorts – and every single one is wearing a cycling helmet.

A whistle blows and all hell breaks loose: men and women run at full pelt onto the neatly groomed lawn, dodging through a multitude of brightly coloured objects until they find the one that belongs to them and unfold it. Click, snap, spin – up come the handlebars, up comes the saddle, round come the wheels. Bike assembled, they mount and head for the track. This is the inaugural Brompton World Championship, now an annual event that demonstrates how celebrated and quirky this ingenious little invention is.

A bicycle has always been a vehicle of freedom, but Andrew Ritchie wanted to build a machine that would give the rider even more. He built a folding bicycle, but not like the clunky, uncomfortable, impossible-to-carry-when-folded versions that had previously found their way onto the market. His would be the best, most human-friendly folding bicycle ever made.

With initial ideas sketched on scraps of paper, the first prototype was developed in 1975 in the bedroom of Ritchie's London flat, overlooking the imposing Brompton Oratory from which it took its name. An obsessive and a perfectionist, it took Ritchie a year to create his vision: a bike that would give its rider the freedom of being able to take it anywhere and everywhere. If a bicycle could be folded to little more than the size of its 16-inch wheels, it could slot into any space in life: beneath an office desk, in an under-stairs cupboard or next to a bar stool. It would fit in the boot of a car, the hold of a yacht, the cloakroom of a theatre and the overhead luggage rack of a train. But it wasn't just about ingenuity in the design; it also needed to ride well, to be comfortable for potentially long distances and to be able to carry at least a briefcase. Nowhere should be off-limits to the rider.

Ritchie's first offering was crude and basic, and wouldn't win any awards for engineering, but it worked. The business launched with 50 bikes: 30 had been pre-ordered, and Ritchie was convinced there had to be another 20 people willing to buy one. The price tag was £250 and all 50 sold straight away.

For the first couple of years, the bicycles were sold as they were made. With a staff of just one, it was exhausting work. In two years he made and sold 500 bikes, breaking even but not able to expand. The design gradually evolved but problems were plentiful: the manufacturer of the hinges went out of business and the frames of the initial bicycles snapped after a few years. Struggling to raise capital, and with the bicycle industry in decline, his timing couldn't have been worse. Manufacturing stuttered to a halt. He pinned his hopes on a partnership with Raleigh, but they rejected him.

Many were the times when Ritchie felt like giving up. He juggled several part-time jobs to sustain the project. But in 1986 a backer came forward and from there, things began to snowball. Production proper finally began under a railway arch in Brentford. With a full-scale operation, it turned a profit from day one. Twenty years later, Brompton has 240 staff making bicycles at a rate of one every three minutes. Ritchie's obsession, perfectionism and perseverance paid off: his bikes are of renowned high quality, commanding a hefty price tag which, as any Brompton owner will tell you, is worth every penny.

Brompton is still 100 per cent British, manufactured in West London to Ritchie's exacting standards. All the bikes are hand-built and customers can choose from millions of different permutations of handlebars, colour, lighting set-up and gears to have a truly original bike.

And the freedom of which he dreamed has been discovered by the thousands of people who each day unfold their bicycle and reveal a world of possibilities. For it's not just the accessory of the commuter: Bromptons are used for leisure, tourism, long-distance riding and even racing. They have been ridden to the summit of Mont Ventoux, on 100+ mile sportives and at the South Pole. World-wanderer Heinz Stücke completed the final 60,000 km of his 50-year world travels on a Brompton, attracted by the ease with which it could be carried on other forms of transport. And every year, hundreds of riders compete in the Brompton World Championship. Despite all the setbacks, Ritchie's perseverance led to his bike becoming a household name and realising his original dream: 'to make a magic carpet you can keep in your pocket'.

Caren Hartley – Making beautiful frames

I suppose it's the jeweller in me. After function, most important is the finishing and the attention to detail.

A flame flares, reflected in a brazer's dark glasses; metal appears as glass under the torch's scorching heat and a bronze filler flows into the join. Around the workshop, bicycle frames hang, some ready to be painted and others yet to take shape. Those that are finished bear the name 'Hartley'.

A jewellery maker and sculptor by training, Caren Hartley loved working with metal: the feel, the smell and the magic of brazing two pieces together to make something new and strong – something that could be used. But working in sculpture, few of her creations, though beautiful, were useful. As she rode her bicycle back and forth to her studio,

Caren pondered that desire, the satisfaction she was lacking in her work. Then it struck her – of course! A bicycle was a metal object – that's what she could make.

The first bicycle that Caren built for herself was a revelation. With every angle carefully calculated and every joint painstakingly constructed, the result was a vehicle she could absolutely trust, a machine where loving care had been devoted to every centimetre. A roadster, compact to suit her 5'4" frame, that first bicycle was called the Pocket Rocket. It fitted her perfectly, handling precisely and reliably. Caren took the bike on a tour to the south of France and proved its worth by climbing each of the three different ascents of Mont Ventoux in one day.

Caren had found her passion, to make something from scratch, to be responsible for the design and creation of a vehicle from beginning to end. It's a niche sector, worlds away from the production lines in the Far East on which the majority of bicycles on the market are manufactured. To hand-build a bicycle takes time, especially those that are custom-made. Inspired by the likes of Hetchins and Holdsworth, the firms making intricately decorative frames in London in the 1930s, her workshop has little electric machinery.

After only 18 months in the business, Caren won her first award: the Best Utility Bike at Bespoked, the handmade bicycle show. She was the first woman ever to win. Tasked by photographer Camille McMillan to create a bike strong enough to carry his photography equipment over the Pyrenees, but with enough shock absorbency that it wouldn't get shaken to pieces, she built the 'Porkeur': a hybrid of the classic *porteur* – a utility bicycle with a front rack that emerged post-war to carry stacks of newspapers around the streets of Paris – and modern fat bike, with balloon tyres more than capable of absorbing the shocks of the road.

Caren is one of only a handful of female frame builders around the world; others include Natalie Ramsland from Portland, Oregon, and Liz Colebrook of Beaumont Bicycle in Shropshire. Though times are changing, the world of frame building is still largely a man's domain, but for Caren it's not much of an issue. 'Maybe it would have been ten years ago,' she says, 'but now most people are more interested in the building of the bike rather than the sex of the builder.'

What matters most is the quality of her work: to make a bicycle that functions to a high standard and looks perfect – one can't exist without the other. For that's why she came into this industry: to allow others to feel that same joy she herself felt when riding her own first purpose-built bicycle. It's about making something of such quality that it's a pleasure to ride and of such beauty that the owner falls in love.

Colin Tonks – Making electricity

Human power is not only a clean and fun method of generating electricity, it's also an amazing way to promote sustainability, exercise and energy appreciation.
ELECTRICPEDALS.COM

For many of us, electricity is a mystery, something that magically appears at the flick of a switch. We might give little thought to the specifics of how it is made but generating your own electricity is not as difficult as you might think; it can even be done by bike. Take a motor, such as the one used in an electric scooter: a battery powers it, making the wheels of the scooter turn. Invert the whole thing and the turning wheel can make the motor rotate which, instead of using electricity, generates it.

It was after seeing an installation built by the American human powered pioneer David Butcher, in which bicycles were used to power lanterns hanging from a massive oak tree, that Colin Tonks founded his company, Electric Pedals. Bursting with ideas about what could be achieved using pedal power, he felt inspired to spread the message. How simple a concept: generate electricity purely by cycling! It was a straightforward example of cause and effect: with the pedals turning, electricity is made. Stop pedalling and off it goes.

Colin took his company to schools, running workshops which aimed not only to teach about physics but also to raise awareness of energy consumption. With a bank of bicycles mounted on rollers, pupils would power light bulbs, laptops and TVs, feeling how much energy was required to drive each – and how much is wasted by leaving them on unnecessarily. With each cyclist generating around 50W, one pupil might be able to light up a bulb – for a kettle it's more like 40. Imagine the gaggle of students it would take to power the Positive Energy Meal: using a plug-in travel frying pan, the task is to generate enough energy to heat it and then sustain that temperature for the time it takes the chef to cook their meal.

Electric Pedals has been commissioned to light up Christmas trees at London's Southbank Centre, to create art at the Tate Modern, to charge festivalgoers' mobile phones and to project messages about endangered animals on the external walls of the Royal Albert Hall. In 2009 Electric Pedals teamed up with the BBC for an episode of *Bang Goes the Theory*, in which 80 cyclists generated the power for an average home while the family went about their daily activities, unaware of what was going on behind the scenes. Working in shifts, the riders kept the pedals turning, groaning each time someone reached for the kettle. When the power shower was turned on, the troops were rallied and for 20 minutes 80 sets of pedals span furiously. As the day progressed, lights around the house went on and, in combination with discarded laptops, TV watching and cooking, the vacuum cleaner being fired up was the final straw. The surge was too much for the exhausted cyclists and the lights went out. After having been introduced to the army of red-faced pedallers, the family suddenly understood the reality of their power consumption. They vowed to be more energy conscious in the future.

A project in Malawi shifted Tonks's focus from being a novelty venture in schools and at festivals: here was a way in which pedal power could benefit communities. In remote areas with no electricity or fuel for a generator, a mobile cinema kit would allow educational and humanitarian films to be screened. In 2013 Tonks took the Backpack Cinema to show Malawian farmers how to combat the drought brought on by climate change. Every piece of the kit, including the projector, fitted inside a backpack. For most it seemed a miracle.

Pedal-powered cinema is the most popular of Electric Pedals' ventures and is the part of their work of which Tonks is most fond. Pedal-powered cinemas appear regularly at festivals and community events all over Britain. It's like a drive-in, but it's a bike-in where cinemagoers' own bicycles are used to power the performance. With equipment requiring roughly 400 W, it's up to the group of 12 or so cyclists to keep the sound going and the pictures rolling. The magic is in creating something mobile, off-grid and that actively involves the audience. Just don't stop pedalling.

Jenni Gwiazdowski – Making a community

I relax by taking my bicycle apart and putting it back together again.
MICHELLE PFEIFFER

Jenni Gwiazdowski worked in a job that should have ticked all the boxes: a communications assistant for an environmental charity, it was morally responsible, she helped people and it was interesting. But Jenni felt something was missing. Something she couldn't quite put her finger on, until she spotted a gap in the market. A keen cyclist, she had bought a bicycle frame with the intention of building it up herself, but couldn't find anywhere in London to do so. She had neither the tools nor the workshop space to do it herself, but any shop she approached would only offer to do it for her. She was aware of the existence in her native California of spaces called bike kitchens: open workshops where people can work on their own bike under the watchful eye of the resident mechanic. As she cycled back and forth to work, Jenni would pass an empty retail unit. After some investigation she learned that it had been empty for ten years. This was the catalyst Jenni had been waiting for – she decided to turn that unit into a California-style bike kitchen: the London Bike Kitchen (LBK). She quit her job and applied for a loan, which was granted. Ideas became plans.

With a team of dedicated volunteers, Jenni turned the little shop into a fully-functional workshop with tool stations, a mechanical washer and a full-sized diagram of a bicycle on the wall. This was no ordinary bike shop or mechanics studio. Jenni's aim was to empower people, enabling them to fix their own bikes rather than just doing it for them. Knowledge is power; being able to mend your bike increases the likelihood of your riding it, with all the benefits that involves.

> *I could buy the tools but where would I keep them? I would use them so infrequently it's not worth it. So often a bike shop will refuse to lend tools even for something simple like tightening brakes.*

LBK also runs classes about topics including maintenance, touring and wheel building. A popular class is BYOB – build your own bike – where customers are shown how to take their bicycle apart and then build it back up. There are also WAG nights (women and gender-variant) – it's all about removing the macho factor. Women and men are equally good at working with bikes, but it's such a male-dominated industry that sometimes as a woman you just want to be in a no-pressure situation.

LBK has won awards recognising its contribution to the local community and the bicycle community as a whole.

This has been the best part of the project, educating anybody and everybody about all aspects of cycling to make it more accessible. It has given people a platform from which to speak, as well as giving them skills. Her little workshop is slotted into a parade of shops in an area of deprivation. Local residents love the bike kitchen – it gives the place a buzz, and the local kids hang around the shopfront, learning how to mend punctures. Jenni will often fix their bikes for free. The community rallied around to help LBK survive near-eviction when the landlord wanted to sell to build luxury flats.

And when Jenni's bike was stolen (the very bike that inspired the whole project), the people she'd helped over the years clubbed together to buy her a new one. That kind of community spirit is something on which you can't put a price.

Liz and Phil Bingham – Making a business

We will never forget how lucky we were that the stars aligned to allow us to spend a year exploring the world by bike. It was a truly life-changing journey.

Liz and Phil had been on the road for eight months, part-way through a 10,000 km bicycle adventure which would take them from the southernmost tip of Argentina to Peru and then from Canada to Mexico – quite a gamble, as they'd only met six months before leaving, on a blind date. Taking a break at a roadside coffee house on the coastal Peruvian highway, Phil and Liz sipped their drinks as vultures circled overhead. They had ridden from deserts of ankle-deep sand to the

Patagonian Steppe, through city streets and the vertiginous Andes, feeling the effect of altitude sickness and long hours in the saddle – sometimes going for several days without encountering any signs of life. Temperatures had ranged from mid-thirties to those so low that the water in their bottles would freeze solid. Spectacular landscapes greeted them, from mountains to salt lakes, where they would ride for miles feeling the crunch of salt crystals beneath their tyres, and the endless navy sky above.

They'd ridden all these miles in the same few items of kit: a robust but unglamorous collection of merino tops and hard-wearing shorts. Liz had packed only 13 items of clothing and had struggled to even find that, as women-specific cycle outfits were often hard to come by. So often the 'shrink it and pink it' attitude would prevail.

A truck driver pulled up to the roadside cafe, dropping from his cab to the ground before approaching them. They glanced at each other nervously – had they upset him? But he was smiling broadly, the grin lighting up his gruff countenance. '¡Cuidado!' he said: Be careful! '¿Por que?' they asked. 'Toma,' he said, handing Liz a hi-vis gilet. 'Take it. I almost didn't see you when I overtook you back there.'

It was a light-bulb moment for Liz and Phil. The range of clothing available for female cyclists required drastic improvement if even the truckers thought Liz could be better kitted out.

As their adventure continued, their thoughts ran wild. Months of sitting on a bike provides plenty of thinking time. The usual musings on what to cook on their little stove that night and casually discussing how to change the world for the better had expanded to include ideas that could be turned into plans on their return. By the end of the trip they had completely fallen in love with cycling and each other; they knew that the bicycle would remain central to their lives – and Phil proposed. The random meeting with the truck driver had confirmed that women's lot in cycling needed improving, beginning with what they wore, so they returned with a fledgling idea for VeloVixen.

An online retailer, VeloVixen brings together designers and manufacturers of women's clothing. The business has won awards, including Total Women's Cycling award for Best Female Specific Retailer. But that's not all: from day one they have tried hard to build a community, encouraging ever greater numbers of women to get on their bikes and experience the joy of independence, fresh air, exercise and cheap transportation. It's about normalising cycling for women and breaking down barriers.

In the four years that VeloVixen has been up and running, the ratio of men's to women's suppliers has changed from 9:1 to 6:4. The team hosted the VeloVixen Women's Cycling Hub at the 2016 Cycle Show – the UK's largest cycling exhibition. It was when Olympic cyclist Jo Rowsell sat on the stage speaking to a packed house that Liz and Phil really grasped the impact their company had had.

'We didn't over-analyse the challenge ahead when we set out on our bike ride – we quickly learnt that a ride like ours helps to simplify life down to very basic requirements.

'By contrast, setting up and running a successful small business is quite the opposite! But it is exhilarating. We're lucky to be able to work in a world in which our passion remains as strong as ever.'

CHAPTER EIGHT
RIDING FOR REHABILITATION

Graeme Willgress – Riding to recovery

*Three years ago, I couldn't imagine cycling anywhere.
Today, I can't imagine not cycling everywhere.*

Graeme Willgress was an active child, excelling at sports and enjoying the outdoor life, but he suffered a mental breakdown at the age of 17 as a result of low self-esteem, anxiety, and being put down by teachers and his tyrannical father. As he bottled up his experiences and his anger, his adult life became dogged by panic attacks, extreme anxiety and bouts of depression. With two marriages behind him and multiple house moves, he rarely felt settled. In his forties he suffered another horrendous breakdown, exacerbated by losing his mother, father and sister – all within three years. Things had reached boiling point.

Graeme shut himself away in his caravan. It was impossible to leave – simply going to the shops was a Herculean task. He felt stigmatised by his local community, separated from his family and friends, and completely isolated from the world.

After a chance meeting with some touring cyclists, he remembered how much he had enjoyed riding in the past, thinking back to happier times mountain biking in Snowdonia as a student; despite the physical effort, he'd found it calming.

So Graeme set out to see if he could recapture some of that tranquillity. He purchased a bicycle and, after a 20-year gap, began to ride again. His first ride was a physically demanding 10 miles through the hills of West Devon. Aside from the fitness, he realised he would need a better bike, but just a short ride had been exactly what he'd needed. 'By the time I got to my house I was completely exhausted… but there was a big smile. I felt I'd achieved something.'

He began going for longer rides – things wouldn't always go smoothly, but steadily he built up the miles and the strength.

> Once I began to cycle I entered a new world… I never felt bad when out on the bike.

Cycling enabled Graeme to begin reconnecting with people. He could turn up at a cycling cafe and just be a cyclist; he could leave his house behind and be free in the world. Becoming a Sustrans ranger for his local stretch of National Cycle Network gave him focus and new friends.

An idea that had lingered in the back of his mind was fighting its way forward: what if he could take a longer ride, a challenging ride, for multiple days? He lived near the sea, and his work with Sustrans had shown him how many coastal cycle paths there were. What if he could ride around the whole thing? The thought thrilled and terrified him in equal measure. Could he do it? Ideas became plans and, with the encouragement of his therapist, Graeme set in motion what would be an incredible journey: Ride2Recovery, which would take him around the coast of mainland Britain. It would be a substantial ride of multiple months but, crucially, without needing to cross the sea. 'The coastline was the limit of what my mind could cope with. I couldn't stretch that boundary any further.'

In 2011, two years after Graeme had conceived of Ride2Recovery, he left his home in Hatherleigh with Irene the bike, Trevor the trailer and enough kit to keep him going for four months. He had completed a few shorter rides in preparation for the challenge that lay ahead. He had also set up a fundraising site for Sustrans, started a blog, and received the nod from his doctor and therapist. Tears rolled down his face as he rolled away from home.

For the next four months, Graeme took it one day at a time. He learned to listen to his body and his mind, to go when it was good and rest when it wasn't. By the end of the first month he was calm, open, stable and, above all, happy. He kept a daily travel diary and discovered a passion for writing, which would help him in the healing process. He returned from his trip having cycled 4,000 miles around the coast of England, Scotland and Wales, but having gone a whole lot further in his steps to recovery.

Since that ride, Graeme has completed two more Ride2Recovery adventures, cycling 2,500 miles along the Atlantic coast from Land's End to John o'Groats, via Ireland, the Outer Hebrides and Shetland. Significantly, the journey involved a flight to Ireland and a ferry to Shetland – modes of transport that had once induced panic attacks and would have been inconceivable only a few years before. His second ride was to France, his first journey in a non-English speaking country for over ten years.

Graeme still battles with poor mental health and episodes of depression and anxiety. But cycling has transformed his life, making his illness manageable, and things he once thought were beyond him are now possible thanks to his two wheels.

'Every time I ride I smile and every time I smile I get a little better.'

Charlotte Roach – How cycling fixed a broken athlete

Basically, if you ride a bike, you are going to fall off. I just came off at the wrong time.

Charlotte Roach was an aspiring triathlete. Since the age of three, when she asked for swimming lessons for her birthday, she had wanted to be an Olympian. An international runner at the age of 17, by the time she was 20 she had joined the British trigold scheme: a fast-track programme that could have led to being selected for the 2012 London Olympic Games. Cycling was new to Charlotte but she was focussed, hard-working and determined – and she wasn't afraid to push herself to the very limits of her capabilities.

Soon after joining the squad, the team were taking part in a regular Sunday training session. Charlotte was slipstreaming the cyclist in front, their wheels overlapping as they accelerated towards a climb. All it took was a small swerve and Charlotte was catapulted into the middle of the road – and into the path of an oncoming Land Rover. She suffered 12 broken vertebrae, punctured lungs, multiple broken ribs and a broken collarbone. 'I remember flying through the air but I never hit the ground,' Charlotte said. 'I was the only person in the scene who didn't think I was going to die.'

Charlotte survived the crash and what followed can only be described as a remarkable recovery. She showed the same focus and determination that she'd applied to her sport, pushing herself beyond what most people can imagine, still desperate to make the Olympic team. In the week following surgery, she was unable to breathe on her own, get out of bed unaided and walk to the toilet, but she kept trying and forced herself to work through the pain. Doctors had thought she would be in intensive care for two weeks; she was home in ten days. Six months after being picked up off the road, Charlotte was competing in an international triathlon. Metalwork was holding her spine together and her collarbone was still broken so badly that her shoulder hung from her body.

She'd taught herself to breathe, walk, swim and run again – but cycling still caused her problems. She was haunted by the crash and hung back in training sessions for fear of falling or being hit again. Frustrated, she continued to push herself. 'In my mind I had to overcome my cycling fears and get back to the start line as quickly as possible. Every day I would wake up with agony in my back and continue my extreme training programme.'

However, a body that has been broken so badly can only be pushed to the limit for so long. After a second round of painful and invasive spinal surgery, Charlotte began to question herself. She'd reached such a high level by consistently working hard in every training session and letting nothing stop her, but now her single-minded goal of an Olympic medal struck her as selfish. For the first time in her life she thought about all the things she couldn't do, like exploring the world and travelling, and actually taking time for herself at weekends. She had only one life to live, and maybe that life was not one of an athlete. So she made the decision to leave the sport.

She began cycling for fun, discovering the joy of riding with no schedule. Free of a training regime, there was nothing to stop her exploring. That summer Charlotte taught in a school in China – what better challenge than to cycle home, fundraising for the air ambulance that had saved her life?

There followed a six-month journey across three continents, through China, the Himalayas, Thailand, Laos, Malaysia, Australia, Turkey, Greece, Italy and France. She was sometimes joined by friends and at other times she rode alone. In Asia she battled with traffic; in Australia she battled with headwinds; and in Europe she battled with herself.

Not finding the strength to go on, nor the courage to quit... I know I simply have to finish this.

Two years and two months after her life-changing accident, Charlotte arrived in Greenwich Park, surrounded by friends and family. She had cycled 8,850 miles and raised almost £10,000 for the air ambulance.

Before the crash, she had been a risk taker, scarcely considering how her actions might affect her or those around her. After the accident, she was scared of everything, overthinking things and seeing danger everywhere. She had tried to ignore it in her blinkered mission to chase her Olympic dream, but it wouldn't go away.

After six months on a bike, experiencing unpredictable traffic, unwelcome attention from strangers, unusual landscapes and harsh terrain – with hour upon hour of thinking time, having to just get on with it alone – she was able to forget her fear.

Perhaps more significantly, her trip finally allowed her to see that the journey shouldn't be forgotten in pursuit of a goal. 'I wondered whether I was ever happy as an athlete, always on a mission for something more and never satisfied with the now. I never questioned the process. The accident made me understand my own mortality. My cycle trip was my first step. It gave me a wake-up call that I had to live my life for today and not for tomorrow.'

Phil Jones – From obesity to Sky Ride leader

Getting on a bike saved my life.

The crowd was roaring: 60,000 pairs of eyes were watching Team GB enter the packed Olympic Stadium in London

2012. Five hundred athletes dressed in white and gold tracksuits walked out, led at the front by cyclist Chris Hoy, holding aloft the Union Flag. On his sofa in Cumbernauld, just outside Glasgow, Phil Jones watched. He wasn't a cyclist. Aged 45 and weighing 23 stone, he hadn't been on a bike for ten years. A taxi driver, the most exercise he ever did was walking down the drive to his cab.

A week earlier, Phil had visited his doctor. The GP had been stern with him: 'Have you heard of fatty liver disease? You're at high risk from diabetes, heart attack and stroke. If you reach the age of 50, you'll be very lucky.'

Watching Hoy and the team, something stirred inside Phil. He had been morbidly obese for the last 20 years and he became aware that this would probably be his last ever Olympics. The sudden realisation made tears roll down his cheeks. *I used to always be on my bike*, he thought, remembering a childhood in Portsmouth spent riding up and down the seafront with his mates.

The very next day he went to the shed and hauled out his bike. It was rusty, the tyres were flat and the rubber cracked, and the frame was covered in cobwebs. So he gave it a good wash, pumped up the tyres and headed out for his first ride, round the block, no more than a mile. He was in the lowest gear almost straight away. He heaved at the pedals, struggling to breathe, his stomach bouncing off his knees and his heart pounding in his ears. Phil returned exhausted and slightly disappointed; he'd imagined jumping on his bike, spinning down the road and feeling great. Although this was clearly going to be much harder than he'd thought, he was completely determined: he could ride a bike, and this was going to be how he took control of his life.

For the next few days, Phil went out for his ride around the block. Each time, his breathing became more controlled, his joints loosened up and his muscles were forced into action. As winter approached, he realised that he risked losing focus so he booked himself a place on the Glasgow to Edinburgh ride the following September and also, as extra motivation, a place on the London to Brighton the following June. As the weeks went by, the weight began to fall off. In four months he had hit his target of being under 20 stone.

Cycling became Phil's life. His weight continued to drop and by the time the Glasgow to Edinburgh ride came along, he had lost 8 stone. He volunteered for a local bike recycling charity, joined a cycling club and trained to become a ride leader for the national Sky Ride programme; riding had done so much for him that he wanted to enable others to experience the same benefits. He was active and happy, no longer wheezing to the top of the stairs or unable to walk for more than a few minutes at a time. He went back to his doctor to ask if he could come off his tablets, adding, 'Actually, I've not been taking them for a month now.' Phil had never heard his doctor swear until that moment. After measuring his blood pressure and weight, his GP agreed that he was healthy.

On his annual renewal as a Sky Ride leader, Phil requested a new jersey. 'My 2XL no longer fits,' Phil wrote. 'Shall we send an XL?' came the response. 'No, a Medium.' Almost straight away, the phone rang. 'Is that Mr Jones? This is Team Sky. We'd like to hear your story...'

Phil was invited to make a documentary about his remarkable transformation. The footage would be shot on club runs and at the Glasgow Velodrome, the track where

Chris Hoy had trained in the years leading up to that fateful Olympics. Phil took the film crew backstage to the athletes' area to show them where Hoy stored his bike. While he spoke to the camera, a man walked up behind him, wheeling his bike towards his locker: Sir Chris Hoy. The shock as Phil came face to face with his hero was palpable. Words failed him and tears pricked his eyes. He stood dumbfounded for several seconds; then he took Chris Hoy's hand in his and shook it. 'Thank you,' he said, 'thank you. You saved my life.'

Together the two men rode the track, Hoy coaching Phil to ride the steep banking of the velodrome. Phil raised both arms in the air as they came to the end of the session. Never had he imagined, while watching that Olympics, that two years later he would be there, riding with the very man who had inspired him to change his life.

'For me, cycling is the answer. I am approaching my 50th, the year my GP said I might not see, full of confidence for the future. I am fitter than I have ever been in my life. I used to live in a dark place. Now I live in the light.'

Nan Little – Taking control of Parkinson's

If I stopped cycling, I'd probably just fade away.

Dr Nan Little, a retired anthropologist from Seattle, has Parkinson's disease. When she was diagnosed in 2008, her right arm hung stiff and painful at her side, the fist clenched, a tremor in her hand. She leaned forward when she walked, shuffling along, unable to raise or turn her head without pain, looking at the pavement rather than the landscape. She lost her sense of smell. Her symptoms puzzled her and she became depressed, anxious and apathetic.

Two and a half thousand miles away, in the US state of Ohio, Dr Jay Alberts was undertaking a study at the Centre for Neurological Restoration, looking at the effects of cycling on Parkinson's patients. It had been a chance discovery during the annual RAGBRAI (Register's Annual Great Bike Ride Across Iowa) that had led to the study: a keen cyclist, Alberts was participating in the week-long, 460-mile ride with a group that included his friend Cathy, who suffered with Parkinson's, and her husband. The couple had arrived on a tandem but it soon became clear that they were not best suited to ride it together. Stepping in to save the situation, Alberts rode with Cathy for the week. His pedal motion was quicker than Cathy's husband's had been: he was forcing her to pedal faster than she would otherwise have done. As the week went on, Alberts and the other participants noticed that Cathy's symptoms seemed to improve. Cathy was amazed. 'Jay! It doesn't feel like I have Parkinson's when I'm on the bike!'

Nan Little heard of Dr Alberts and the success of his trial: there had been a 35 per cent improvement in the patients who had undertaken forced exercise, specifically fast-paced cycling: riding at a cadence of 80–90 rpm. For the first time she realised she might be able to do something about her condition other than relying solely on medication, whose side effects included anxiety attacks and compulsive behaviours. In her case this meant incessant cross-stitch – it might have produced lots of pretty artwork, but was exhausting for her and her husband when it involved waking in the middle of the night and cross-stitching for hours.

So Nan worked with Dr Alberts on a cycling regime, with a mind to also take part in RAGBRAI. 'Fast-paced cycling increases brain function which seems to ease the symptoms of PD,' explained Dr Alberts. Motivated by the thought of that 460-mile ride, Nan pushed herself far beyond what he suggested and she began riding four, five, six days a week – anything from an hour and a half to four hours each time.

Exactly a month after beginning the programme, Nan was out walking her dogs. She noticed that both her arms were swinging freely. She stopped and uncurled her right hand, which stayed uncurled. She turned her head left and right, and then rolled it all the way round: no pain. Nan stood there on the pavement and cried.

She went to see her doctor. 'If I didn't know you had Parkinson's, I wouldn't diagnose it,' he said. Over the next few months she was able to halve her medication.

Nan managed her ride across Iowa. She went on to complete five more RAGBRAIs and each subsequent year has taken on a different challenge: to climb Mt Kilimanjaro, to reach Annapurna base camp in the Himalayas, to trek to Machu Picchu on the Inca Trail in Peru and to explore the Canadian Rockies. Her doctor believes she's probably the strongest 70-year-old woman in the US. Nan says:

> When I cycle, my brain works better, up to several weeks after stopping. No medicine works so long.

It has made a huge difference to her emotionally as well as physically, with the sense of empowerment that comes with knowing she can work through whatever challenges Parkinson's throws at her.

She still has to take medication, but cycling is now an integral part of her life. 'I have continued to deteriorate over the years, but at a much slower pace than predicted. I have my body back. I can get on the bike and forget about other things that are going on around me, any pains or anxieties. Instead of contemplating my cane or my wheelchair, I have my bicycle.'

Tommy Scargill – Riding against cancer

I didn't want to be defined by my cancer,
but I felt as though I was being chased by
death. I needed to start chasing life.

Tommy was just four when he had his first bout of cancer: acute lymphoblastic leukaemia. Young enough not to remember, but old enough for chemotherapy, he asked, 'Why am I feeling sick all the time, Mummy?' The cancer returned when he was 14 years old and this time it was much more memorable: hair falling out, wretched sickness, the curious looks at school, the worry etched on his parents' faces, the days of endless hospital corridors and doctors' appointments and medication.

Out of remission, when Tommy was 18 he collapsed on the football field. There was a problem with his heart after all the chemotherapy; further medication saw his energy levels plummet and depression take hold.

Desperate to escape the downward spiral, Tommy went travelling, discovering a love for life on the road. But when he returned, so did the blues; he felt trapped, caught up in the monotony of life, and depressed by the endless daily routine of work and sleep, which was not helped by the lingering side-effects of his medication. Adventure was in his blood, and he needed to get out there again and do something. But money was tight, so Tommy trawled Instagram in search of inspiration and noticed a theme: most of the people travelling were doing so on a bicycle. He had a bike. Although he hadn't ridden it for a few years, he knew this was the answer he'd been looking for. Cycling would give him valuable time to be himself, away from the worries and concern of others; he'd be free to discover new landscapes, new cultures, new people, and to experience that butterfly feeling again – then he would know he was alive.

'I'm going to China,' he told his friends, 'and I'm going to cycle there.'

'But it's so far!' they said. 'It's too hard. You are ill. Don't exert yourself.'

Tommy had made up his mind. He wasn't an outdoorsy man, yet he would be camping and foraging along the way. He was not even a cyclist, yet he would be riding several thousands of miles. The whole point was getting out of his comfort zone, having new experiences. Yes, it might be dangerous, but staying in his current life would be lethal.

In the autumn of 2015 he found himself in a field in West Wales, cycling along an avenue lined with 200 people egging him on as if their lives depended on it. This was his big moment: the grand depart, from Yestival, a gathering whose mantra is 'Say Yes More' – a festival of positivity set up by adventurer Dave Cornthwaite to encourage people to live their dreams.

> *There are days in our lives that we never forget, and that day, for Tommy, will be one of them.* He had made it to the end of one journey, a journey of planning and decision-making and departure from his previous life, and was about to begin another. When one person shares their important moments with so many others, they create change without realising it.

Tommy now lives on the road, steadily making his way towards China. Though this path may be paved with challenges, travel has given him a fundamental belief in the goodness of the world and a zeal for finding it. It's impossible not to be changed by such a life; initially shy and nervous, Tommy has become more open, more willing to speak and ask for help, and more convinced of the benefit of talking and sharing problems. 'We are stronger together than alone,' he writes. After trying to please everyone else, he is now happy to be himself, not to take life too seriously and to rejoice in the small things. 'Smile,' he says. 'It might just make someone smile back.'

By chasing life, Tommy has found a profound happiness. The road taught him things that he could never learn in school – the world is the best school there is: learning, experiencing, broadening horizons. 'With my bike I'm free,' he says. 'Don't just exist. Live.'

Breifne Earley – From the depths of despair to World Cycle Race champion

Cycling is like a drug, but with only positive side effects.

Breifne Earley had battled with depression for much of his adult life. In his late twenties his mental health deteriorated after spending a 70-hour working week under the watchful eye of a negative boss. As his work environment grew more hostile, the other parts of his life became a struggle. Overweight, lonely and depressed, relationships with his girlfriend, his family and his friends grew strained.

One evening in October 2010 Breifne decided to end his life. He had reached that unimaginable low, where he could no longer see a way forward and suicide was the only way out. Two distinct things prevented him from acting, though: an invitation to his cousin's memorial service and watching the movie *The Bucket List*. Stirred into action, Breifne wrote his own list. The date of his cousin's memorial was 10 October 2010: 10/10/10. Over the next 13 months, until 11/11/11, he lost 5 stone, went on 50 blind dates, learned to swim and cook, changed career, performed in ten open mic nights, saved 10 per cent of his salary, cycled around New Zealand, faced his open water swimming fears, competed in triathlons and ran a marathon.

Setting himself challenges had increased Breifne's ability to deal with the little things thrown up by life. His mental health was in good shape. He wanted to undertake an even greater challenge: 'Something huge, something difficult, even impossible, something I could be proud of until the day I die.' He entered the World Cycle Race: he would attempt to ride solo and unsupported around the world. It was an incredible ambition for someone who, until his recent discovery of a love for cycling, hadn't been on a bike for over a decade. He knew he wouldn't be as fast as the other competitors, but he could be as tough. He would simply spend longer in the saddle than they did.

In March 2014 Breifne met the three other competitors who would be racing him around the globe and set off on a journey that would completely change his life. Tackling the challenge of the road he found an inner strength he had never known before. Finding places to stay at each step, securing funding, dealing with mechanical issues and eventually continuing when all the other participants had withdrawn or been disqualified, made his confidence soar. Those seminal moments of crossing the Great Divide on Route 66 or climbing Baldwin Street, the world's steepest street, in Dunedin, New Zealand would remain with him for the rest of his life. The folk who gave him food, drink, company and a bed, each one treating him identically no matter where in the world they lived, reminded him that it's we who manufacture the differences between us. After hundreds of hours of self-therapy with only his thoughts for company he crossed Tower Bridge, 490 days and 18,000 miles after leaving to become the World Cycle Race winner.

'My life is unrecognisable since finishing the race. I don't sweat the small stuff anymore.'

> *The arrival back in Ireland and my hometown in Leitrim in particular left me speechless.*

The warmth and support from my country was phenomenal.

'I was at the lowest imaginable point the evening I made the decision to take my own life. Now I enjoy every moment I have.'

Jasmine Reese – Learning life's lessons

Cycling taught me a lesson that school and society could not.

From the moment Jasmine first picked up the violin, she dreamed of being a professional musician. Her talent was obvious but she never felt good enough. Having come to it relatively late, at the age of 12, she felt that she'd started on the back foot. She was a perfectionist, with an unhealthy fear of failure and a crushing voice of self-doubt about her abilities. 'For years, that voice slept with me, ate dinner with me and sat on the scroll of my violin as I practised and performed.' She became depressed and agoraphobic: she skipped classes and wouldn't leave her room.

While searching the internet, one day Jasmine stumbled across bicycle tourism. Overnight, she made a decision to cycle across the USA. It would be her escape from the prison she felt her life had become and would help to combat the weight gain induced by her depression. She fought against the voice of doubt questioning her decision. Cycling? She'd never been active in her life! As a plus-size girl, how would she find cycle clothing that fit? Would her bicycle be able to support her weight? And what about her dog? Fiji was a rescue dog, originally intended for her mum, but she had chosen Jasmine, padding down the stairs each night to whimper at her door. There was no question that Fiji wouldn't come.

She ignored the voice and planned her trip – food, accommodation and route – and as soon as she took to the road, the inner critic was silenced. She felt empowered. She was finally doing something over which she had complete control: there was no society frowning upon her or causing her to question whether she was good enough. She could accomplish anything. She was no longer in a rush, no longer comparing herself to her peers, bowing to the pressure of being a good violinist in a specified amount of time. The clock ticking above her head was gone. The phrase 'Slow and steady wins the race' became her mantra; her determination to continue with her music was renewed. If she could cycle every day for hours on end, then she could practise the violin.

Though she hated exercise, she adored cycling – it was the perfect way to travel, at a pace dictated by her strength and the road: a journey between destinations with exercise as a bonus. It wasn't always easy, but hills were a metaphor for life: she would have to get over them in order to see the next great thing. She encountered good days and bad days, and sometimes she would have to wait out the storm – a valuable lesson in patience. She learned to embrace the challenge and experience, rather than focussing purely on the end point; a lesson that would equally apply to her pursuit of a career as a violinist.

However, she really struggled in the first few days with Fiji, as her dog did not take kindly to the road. Her comfortable routine had been disrupted; she felt unsettled and anxious, and growled all the time. She barked at passers-by; she barked at the hosts Jasmine had arranged to stay with. She refused to sit down in the trailer and, by poking her head out, would overbalance the whole thing and throw Jasmine from her bike. Just four days into the journey, Jasmine was on the verge of asking her mum to come and collect Fiji. But just outside Philadelphia, they came across a beautiful trail so Jasmine let Fiji out of the trailer and allowed her to run. As soon as the dog was in the fresh air, her temperament changed. She loved running! She stopped barking and listened to her owner: Jasmine had to trust her, and she would be trusted in return. Fiji loved the exercise; she enjoyed being outdoors, with all its new smells – things to explore and rabbits to chase – and meeting an entire nation of people who would give her treats. She was a running dog, a travelling dog, a road dog.

Jasmine returned home after having cycled 1,000 miles from New York to California. She was 30 lbs lighter, sure of herself and determined to accomplish her musical goals. She followed that trip by setting off on a world tour with her two most treasured companions: Fiji and her violin. In each place she reaches, she gives street performances and collaborates with local musicians. Jasmine has achieved her dream: she is playing her violin all over the world.

Phil Southerland – Beating diabetes

Anything is possible, even if you have diabetes.

There are many things that lead us to ride bikes, but for Phil Southerland it was the desire to eat a chocolate bar. He'd lived with diabetes for his entire life, learning at the age of six how to check his glucose level and give himself insulin injections. Sweets and treats were banned in his house. But for a 12-year-old boy the temptation was too great: he sneaked his first bar and his blood sugar went through the roof. Guilty, and a little scared, Phil took himself outside for a hard bike ride, hoping it might help. It did, dramatically: his blood sugar returned almost at once to normal, as the exercise helped his body to absorb the insulin. So he decided to go for longer rides, earning himself the ability to eat more chocolate, counting the hours until he could have another bar. After a while he began riding for the sake of the ride, not the chocolate. He made friends through cycling; he was really good at it. He'd stumbled across the sport by accident, but it became a passion.

Phil had been just seven months old when his mother first rushed him to the Emergency Room with suspected diabetes: the youngest recorded case in the world at that time. Doctors warned her that Phil was at risk from organ failure and diabetic coma in the short term, and there was a likelihood that he would develop blindness, kidney failure, cardiovascular disease or nerve damage as he reached adulthood. He had actually been warned off cycling by the doctor, as something which might complicate his blood sugar control.

But in Phil's experience, cycling had vastly improved his health, and by the age of 19, he was racing for his college. After one training session, he was approached by another cyclist, Joe Eldridge, who had noticed Phil injecting. Joe was also diabetic, but was struggling; he allowed sport to interrupt what should have been an orderly insulin ritual, his chaotic approach far different to Phil's careful monitoring. They became friends and set a challenge: whoever had the highest blood sugar would have to buy dinner. Usually it was Joe. After three months, Joe had brought his blood sugar levels under control and Phil was the one footing the bill.

The pair dreamed of racing professionally so in 2005 they set up Team Type 1, the world's first pro team including cyclists with diabetes. That year the team won the Race Across America (RAAM).

In December 2012 they joined forces with Novo Nordisk, a Danish pharmaceutical company manufacturing synthetic insulin – every athlete in Team Novo Nordisk has diabetes. From humble beginnings, they grew to include a men's professional team, development team, junior team, tri team, women's team, running team and Type 2 team. The entire project includes nearly 100 athletes racing with diabetes. By 2020, the 100th anniversary year of the discovery of insulin, the pro team hopes to reach the Tour de France.

Cycling not only helps with the management of diabetes, but it is also liberating. Every day can be different for someone with diabetes and regular exercise can really assist in this challenge. It doesn't have to be a 160 km bike ride – it can be a walk, a football game or a swim.

As Phil says, 'In an age where there's a pill for everything, exercise is the billion dollar drug that never gets prescribed.'

CHAPTER NINE

MARVELLOUS MADNESS

Rob Holden – Up Mont Ventoux on a Boris Bike

*The Ventoux is a god of Evil... It extracts
an unfair tribute of suffering.*
ROLAND BARTHES, FRENCH PHILOSOPHER AND BICYCLE RACING FAN

All good ideas begin, as they say, over a glass of something –
usually alcoholic – but in Rob Holden's case, it was an innocent
cup of coffee taken on a break during a regular Sunday ride.
Speaking to his friends Matt Winstone and Ian Laurie, the
conversation turned to the hire bikes in London, dubbed 'Boris
Bikes' after Boris Johnson, the mayor when the scheme was
launched. The bikes run on a timer, and after 24 hours a charge
of £150 is applied. 'How far do you reckon you could go with
a Boris Bike in twenty-four hours?' asked Ian. 'I dunno...
South of France?' Rob replied. 'You'd have to do something
pretty spectacular when you got there to make it worth it.'

'Yeah, like ride up Ventoux!' They laughed, and returned to sipping their coffees.

Rob broke the silence. 'You know, that's not a bad idea...'

Mont Ventoux stands at a magnificent 1,912 m, towering above the village of Bedoin in the south of France. At its peak stands an iconic observation tower, visible from the village, suggesting little of how hard it might be to reach it.

The mountain is renowned as a hard climb – some say the toughest of all the Tour de France climbs. The great Belgian Eddy Merckx required oxygen at the top in 1970 and in 1967 it claimed the life of the English cyclist Tom Simpson, who collapsed 1.5 km from the summit. The climate is just as unforgiving as the 10 per cent average gradient; from sheltered forest, the rider emerges onto slopes where winds howl, sun scorches, rain batters and snow scatters. There is no respite, no relief.

What had started as a joke in a coffee shop turned into a plan. The trio would hire a bike from a docking station in London, put it in the back of their jeep, drive the 720 miles from London to Bedoin (including journeying through the Channel Tunnel on Eurostar), cycle up the mountain, get back in the car and return to London – and all before the 24-hour cut-off time.

People said it couldn't be done. Mont Ventoux is hard enough on a carbon-fibre road bike, let alone one of these city bikes that weighs over 25 kg and has only three gears. Rob had been a good climber as a kid but hadn't done much serious riding for a while: marathons, Ironmans and mountain bike endurance racing was as tough as it got. This was simply ridiculous. 'We didn't really know what we were getting ourselves into,' admitted Matt afterwards.

The day arrived: at 3.58 a.m. Rob removed the bike from its docking point near central London. They had 24 hours to complete the challenge and return the bike. The race was on.

They headed off in the direction of the Channel Tunnel and, despite road closures along the way, made it to the Eurostar on time. Disembarking in France at 7.30 a.m. local time, they arrived eight and a half hours later at the base of the mountain. With no sleep and zero warm-up, Rob mounted the bike and commenced the climb.

'I had no idea how hard or how easy it would be,' he said, beginning the ascent in an optimistic second gear. 'I just took it one kilometre at a time.' Two kilometres later he was in bottom gear. The sustained gradient was draining, sapping his strength and his determination. It was hot on the mountain – roughly 25°C, with no breeze – and the heat soared once Rob emerged from the forest section; the previous week it had snowed, so the winter jersey he had brought along was wholly unsuitable.

> *All the stories say, once you've got to Chalet Reynard, you've cracked it; the steepest part is out of the way. But now, you're tired and you're on the exposed part.*

A few kilometres from the summit, Rob's legs started cramping. He resorted to weaving in zigzags up the road – with not enough power in his legs to get that hunk of a bike to go straight, there was little else he could do. Passing the memorial to Tom Simpson gave him the boost he needed to tackle the final 1.5 km, which was almost the hardest of all.

He reached the summit as the sun sank below the horizon, having climbed 1,612 m in 2 hours and 55 minutes, without stopping once. Drenched in sweat, sleep-deprived, dehydrated and in pain, exhausted relief flooded him. But there was little time to celebrate: they were half an hour behind schedule. They piled the bike back in the car and sped off down the mountain, Rob desperately trying to dry his sweaty, grimy skin and change into clean clothes as Matt flung the truck around the corners in a valiant effort to make up time. But the weather had other ideas.

The heavens opened with a downpour of biblical proportions and the road was soon awash as rain pelted on the windscreen. The atmosphere in the vehicle was tense; they could feel their success slipping away, but was it worth putting everyone in danger? After eight fraught hours of driving, they arrived at Calais – and the Eurostar check-in – with one minute to spare. Theirs was the last car to board before the gate closed.

The train arrived ten minutes late in Folkestone, giving them 1 hour and 10 minutes to get back to the docking point in London. Their satnav gave them an estimated time of arrival as 3.57 a.m.: 1 minute before they would incur the fine.

The rain that had dogged the return journey in France continued; with limited visibility, their speed was restricted and made even slower by an accident, roadworks and numerous red lights.

Eventually, they arrived back in London and at the docking point. 'Come on, come on, come on!' said Matt as the seconds ticked by. The bike came out of the car and into the dock: click, whirr, green light. They'd made it – with 22 seconds to spare.

Ian had made a video of the feat, which went viral. 'What you don't see is me throwing up in the back of the car for two hours from dehydration and because Matt was cornering so fast,' said Rob of the sprint back across France.

'The ride itself was ridiculously hard. With essentially one gear the whole way up, it was a struggle just keeping the pedals turning. By Chalet Reynard my whole body was in pain. Having said all that, we did what we set out to do. The weather was great, the mountain was awe inspiring and I reached the summit at sunset. It was perfect.'

Andrew Hellinga – Cycling backwards

Backwards cycling is harder than forward cycling.

Andrew Hellinga wanted a world record. A member of Challenge for Change, an organisation based in Australia that raises awareness and money for African children, he was looking for a new fundraising stunt. A world record would gain the necessary notoriety and media interest to increase awareness of and donations to his cause, and would satisfy his desire to appear in the famous *Guinness World Records*. It also amused Andrew to enter into some harmless peer rivalry with fellow Aussie and group member Reid Anderton, who had recently set a world record for cycling around Australia. So he started searching for something he could do.

An entry on the Guinness World Records website jumped out at him: cycling backwards. *I could do that*, he thought – as a teenager, he'd learned to sit on the handlebars and ride backwards as a way of impressing his mates. He'd been pretty good at it, too – notwithstanding the time he'd plunged off the edge of Cleveland Pier. The record was 180 km in 24 hours and he decided to give it a go.

His first attempt was a disaster. It had been a good few decades since he'd practised that skill, and it was like learning to balance all over again. His road bike didn't help – it was almost impossible to find a comfortable position to sit on the handlebars, and even less possible to reach the pedals. So he borrowed a smaller, hybrid-style bike from a friend which, while still not as comfortable as sitting on an actual saddle, at least allowed him to propel the thing along.

Next, he needed a straight road with a good surface and few obstacles. He arranged permission with the nearby Motorplex venue to use their 2.1 km circuit to train and attempt the record, but when he arrived there for the first time, the member of staff on duty clearly hadn't been informed. Andrew managed to convince him that, yes, he had permission to use this motor-racing circuit on his pushbike – and then proceeded to amaze him by mounting and riding off backwards. An hour later – and after numerous instances of riding off the track – he had covered 16 km. After three months of training he had raised his average speed to 24 km per hour, and he had successfully ridden 100 km. He was ready.

The day of the challenge arrived. Andrew put on his helmet (backwards), mounted the handlebars and set off, the track abuzz with spectators despite the 6 a.m. start. The heat rose from the tarmac as the day went on, registering 35°C when the sun reached its maximum height. At least he had a cooling breeze – in the form of 60 kph gusts of wind. His friend Reid Anderton joined him for moral support, but managed just one lap before the wind forced him to retire. Andrew kept the pedals turning, backwards, round and round, every so often looking over his shoulder to keep himself on track.

After 10 hours and 15 minutes of riding, Andrew reached 180 km and broke the world record. He jumped down from the bike as the crowd cheered, raised a glass to celebrate, ate an entire pizza and then hopped back onto the handlebars to see how much further he could go. The pressure was off: he could relax. But perching on a tube no more than 2 inches in diameter, with your eyes fixed over your shoulder, is far from relaxing. The heat was relentless and the wind continued to rise. The next four hours were a horrible test of stamina, with exhaustion soon setting in. He stopped a few times and lay on the bitumen, feeling its subtle comfort. When would this day end?

By 10.30 p.m. he was back into his stride – the wind had died down, and he reached the midnight hour steady and sure of himself. The crowds had dissipated but three of his mates took to the track, cajoling and supporting him. The horizon brightened at around 5 a.m. and relief started to flood Andrew: just one more hour to go. People began to arrive to witness the finish and then... disaster! A puncture! A quick change and the wheel was back on.

At 6 a.m. Andrew stopped cycling. He had ridden 337 km backwards and in doing so set two new world records: for the furthest distance cycled backwards in 24 hours and the furthest distance cycled backwards, full stop. It had been a serious test of strength, stamina and endurance. He had raised a substantial amount of money for his charity and received with deep satisfaction his certificate from the Guinness World Records.

'I felt relief, joy and a quiet sense of pride that I had completed something pretty cool.'

Joff Summerfield – A modern Thomas Stevens

*When people see me on my bike, I hope
they think, if he can do that on that crazy
machine, I can face my own challenges. I hope
I inspire people. I leave a trail of smiles.*

It's early May in a cemetery in London, England. Vegetation creeps over the gravel path; the trees glow with a suggestion of summer and between their leaves, dappled light flickers on the moss-covered gravestones below. Against a railing leans an unusual bicycle: one large wheel and one tiny wheel trailing behind, with knapsacks and bags strapped along the length of a gracefully curved frame. A man kneels at a grave and takes a small stone from it. He reads the inscription on the headstone: In loving memory | Thomas Stevens | Born 1855, died 24 January 1935. That man is Joff Summerfield; his bicycle is a replica penny-farthing that he built himself, and he is about to set off around the world in the footsteps of the very man at whose grave he now stands. For Thomas Stevens was the first man to ever cycle the world on a penny-farthing – a journey that no one had since replicated.

How did Joff come to be there, with a bicycle that had been out of manufacture since the 'safety' bicycle arrived in the 1880s to replace it? Joff did not have a long history of cycling, but he had always had a love for antiques, fuelled by his father's passion for restoring pre-war Rolls-Royces and Bentleys. He came to cycling, like many, to save cash when he became self-employed and he soon rediscovered a childhood affection for the bicycle. He rode a pre-war DSA bicycle to Amsterdam for a holiday and loved it so much he decided this would be how he would see the world.

The penny-farthing was as eccentric a bike as he could think to make; Joff had always felt a need to be different. He built himself one after studying those in museums and then taught himself to ride it. He tested it out by cycling it to Paris. He then built another, lighter, one and rode it from one end of Great Britain to the other.

'Anyone can ride a penny,' says Joff. 'It's the getting on and off that's difficult.' He's had his fair share of headers; pitching over the handlebars is common for penny-farthing riders – a pothole is enough to catch the wheel and send the rider hurtling from a great height to the ground. He took the associated broken bones in his stride, riding more and more, discovering a whole movement of modern-day penny riders – some on newly built machines, some on original bikes. He raced at the London Nocturne; he raced at the World Championships, and won. He rode the Spring Classics, cobbles and all – what better bike to ride such historic events than the penny? He now makes penny-farthings and sells them.

His world tour suffered two false starts: the first, just 26 miles from home, when his knee gave in and he couldn't continue. The second time he made it to Budapest before more knee problems forced him to return. But at the third attempt, Summerfield completed his circumnavigation, cycling a total of 22,500 miles. He rode his penny along the banks of the Danube, through the mountains of Southeast

Asia, through the Rajasthan desert and the expansive Australian outback. He rode it along the endless asphalt of the United States highways and through the searing heat of Death Valley – and everywhere he went, people came to see him. Children laughed with delight and adults smiled in surprise. Groups of kids playing football in the street would abandon their game to run with him. Everywhere he went, people smiled. 'People across the world, rich and poor, ride bicycles,' Joff said. But none rode such a bike as this. Folk would stop him so they could take a picture. Joff would always engage them in conversation. That's what travel is all about: the people you meet, the conversations you have.

Joff stayed on the road for two and a half years, exploring the world, riding around 40 miles a day, meeting people, chatting and writing in his journal. On his return to England, he revisited the grave in North London where Thomas Stevens was buried. He replaced the stone he'd taken, a token to the spirit of that great man.

Anne-Sophie Rodet and Kelli Carley – Uni girls kick Alps

Be at one with the universe. If you can't do that, at least be at one with your bike.
LENNARD ZINN

The sight of a unicycle rolling by, the rider balancing atop its solitary wheel, arms outstretched, never fails to raise a smile. It's seen as the preserve of the eccentric, the kind of vehicle that will stop people in their tracks – part intrigue, part amazement, part longing – how on earth do you do that?

For Anne-Sophie Rodet, it's second nature: she's been riding the wheel since the age of five, when her brother began a weekly circus activity and she begged to do the same. A tomboy, it was unicycling rather than the trapeze or tightrope that attracted her.

In unicycling she found a wonderful community and was soon involved in every aspect of the sport: street, trials, freestyle, racing and mountain unicycling. Born and raised at the foot of the French Alps, this was her calling, her passion, and aged 26 she became downhill world champion in her age category.

Long distance touring, though, had never appealed; Anne-Sophie assumed it would be boring. Even so, in 2005 she arranged to meet a group of touring unicyclists when they passed through France: as the President of the French Unicycling Federation at the time, she was intrigued by these 'crazy people on big wheels' (36 inch unicycles were rare). The team were funny, friendly and open – exactly what Anne-Sophie had come to expect from the unicycling community, and their ride seemed more tough than boring. They invited her to join them on their next trip: the Mediterranean Unicycle Tour. Anne-Sophie accepted straight away. Even though it would be an arduous ride, the team would be fantastic.

So the following year she joined nine other unicyclists and rode from Slovenia to the South of France via Croatia, Italy and Corsica: 1,000 km in 19 days. She absolutely loved it. When she returned home, she decided she no longer wanted to take the bus, and started commuting by unicycle.

More tours followed: self-supported, solo endeavours that took her through the ice and snow of the Canadian

Rockies and then 4,600 km across the gravel roads of windy Patagonia. But an adventure closer to home remained at the back of her mind: riding the Haute Route (high route) through the Alps from Chamonix in France to Zermatt in Switzerland, a popular challenge for hikers and cross-country skiers. Setting off from the village in which she grew up, the ride would cover 500 km of trails with around 20,000 m elevation gain and would be something of a homecoming, bringing her back to the place where she had first met that group of touring unicyclists who had sparked all of her adventures in the first place.

Kelli Carley had learned to ride a unicycle when her son told her matter-of-factly that she was too old to learn how to ride. She spent a week mastering the wheel, determined to prove him wrong.

Living in the Colorado mountains, she had soon started exploring the local trails and fell hopelessly in love with the sport. It was on a muni weekend in 2016 – just a handful of months before the Alps trip – that she met Anne-Sophie; when she asked if she'd like to join, Kelli took just two days to say yes.

It would be a huge challenge for Kelli, who had been unicycling for less than two years. In those early days, while exploring her nearby state park, she had found a circuit where two trails met to form a loop, just a mile and a half long: an easy hike, but not so simple for her: 'As a brand new unicyclist, the loop about killed me.' Wheeling between the pines and aspens, her wide tyres stumbling over rocks and dips, and struggling up the climbs, she lost count of how many times she'd had to stop. But as the weeks went by, she went back again and again, each time aiming for fewer breaks and each time finding it a little easier. Her mission was to complete the loop without stopping; after eight months, Kelli finally managed it.

Autumn turned to winter, the ice-slicked trails hidden beneath a flurry of snow. She switched to a studded tyre and rode the route with the wind whipping in her face, her hands numb. As she grew in confidence, she began to explore different trails around the park but would always come back to that little loop, for a progress check or a quick warm-up, eventually flying around it without breaking a sweat.

Shortly before departing from the US for the Alps, Kelli had gone out with a loaded, heavy pack, planning to ride the technical trails which would most closely match the terrain she was about to encounter. But force of habit pulled her towards that little loop, and with her pack hefted onto her back, she began to ride. One lap... two laps... three. 'I never would've imagined that little loop would lead to the Alps. Those laps added up. The perseverance paid off.'

For a month the pair threaded their way through the breathtaking mountain trails of the Alps, riding beneath the August sun along single-track trails, in places the route so steep and rocky that they would have to carry their unicycles on their backs. Each night they made camp beneath the stars, cooking on their tiny stove, and each day they awoke to see the next peak towering in the distance. In each other they had found the perfect expedition partners – and in unicycling, the perfect way to explore those trails.

Alastair Humphreys – Muckle Flugga on a Brompton

Adventure is all around us, at all times.

It's easy to overlook the country in which you live when searching for adventure. It can seem too ordinary, too local, not daring enough. Adventure often implies a foreign shore, an exotic language, somewhere you will find yourself out of your comfort zone; exploring the corners of one's own backyard is often overlooked.

Alastair Humphreys, a National Geographic Adventurer of the Year, has spent most of his adult life hooked on adventure – huge, challenging expeditions that have seen him cycle 46,000 miles around the world, walk across the Empty Quarter desert and row the Atlantic Ocean. But these adventures take time, money, expertise and determination, and the commitment involved is daunting enough to discourage most people from even trying. 'I wish I could do what you do,' people would write. This made him ponder. He was just a normal person – surely others could do the same? 'Adventure is more of an attitude than anything else, and if that's true, surely you can find adventure anywhere.'

So Alastair walked around the M25, the most boring thing he could think to do. It turned out to have as much challenge, excitement, interest and enjoyment as he could have hoped, and it became the first of his trademark microadventures: seeking adventure in places where you least expect it, in short segments of time and without having to spend too much money.

It was while listening to the cricket that Alastair first heard of Muckle Flugga: the northernmost tip of the northernmost island of the UK, a lighthouse sitting on a rock off the coast of Unst in the Shetland Islands – an archipelago with as much beauty as any around the world, but right here in the British Isles. He felt an irrepressible desire to go there.

Together with his friend Joe, he made a plan: to travel the length of Shetland, from Sumburgh Head in the south to Muckle Flugga in the north. The journey would take them over three islands: Mainland, Yell and Unst; they would cycle the land and paddle the straits. The challenge was to find a boat small enough to carry on their bikes, and bicycles small enough to carry in a boat. The answer: inflatable packraft and Brompton.

Wobbling away from Sumburgh Head on Bromptons laden with tents, luggage and packrafts, they headed northwards across Mainland, the largest of the Shetland Islands. The road climbed and fell through farmland and peat bog, through scattered settlements and fishing towns whose harbours buzzed with boats and seagulls. They rode side by side on the A road, where sheep were more common than cars. They laughed at themselves for their ridiculous idea: for riding folding bikes over 70 miles which, with their tiny wheels and compact geometry, are better suited to sit beneath the desk of an office worker in the City. But therein lay the beauty of the adventure. At the shore, once packrafts had been inflated and bicycles reduced to little more than the size of those wheels, they paddled out across Yell Sound.

Adrenaline was high on the crossing: though short, visibility was poor and the currents strong. They arrived on the other side soaked, cold and longing for a shower. But risk, discomfort and physical effort are sometimes what you need. It would make the arrival at Muckle Flugga all the more worthwhile.

Inevitably, the rain came, the clouds descending on their journey through Yell; the tiny island was battered by the wind and the soggy adventurers conceded defeat as they shivered in a pub with their clothes strung out to dry. They were warned of the currents in Bluemull Sound and told that tides of 4 knots could fling their tiny craft wide off the islands and far into the North Sea. There was a perfectly good ferry they could take, the locals said. But the next morning they once again packed their bikes and lashed them to the rafts. The rain had cleared and a deep calm had descended; the pale Scottish sun was smiling down as they paddled gently across the Sound and along the coastline of Unst. The remaining stretch was once more covered by bike – the final 4 km without a road – and they struggled to push their Bromptons through ankle-deep grass as sheep scattered in their wake.

Then there it was: Muckle Flugga lighthouse, crowning a rock across a crystal sea. A green finger of land stretched towards it and that's where they pitched their tents – flat and velvety, it was like camping on a snooker table. The wave-slapped rocks were white with gannets, and puffins eyed them warily from the nearby cliff edge while Shetland ponies sniffed at their bikes. The northern skies darkened, eventually, at 11 p.m.

No matter how much exploring one does, there is always adventure to be had in the most unlikely of places. Alastair has travelled to all corners of the globe by boat, bike and by foot. Yet here, in the extreme point of his home country, was one of the most beautiful campsites he'd ever found.

Jim and Elisabeth Young – A bicycle built for two

*You'll look sweet upon the seat of
a bicycle built for two.*
'DAISY BELL' BY HARRY DACRE

It took two eccentric people to ride an eccentric bicycle across America in the 1930s. Newly married, Jim and Elisabeth Young were silly with love and silly about each other. Their wedding day had been Friday 13. They were described in the *San Francisco Chronicle* as having 'a passion for not settling down'. Finding themselves jobless after a disagreement with their boss (they both worked as journalists for the same magazine), they decided that, instead of seeking work elsewhere, they would cycle across the United States. Jim was a Civil War buff and wanted to visit the seventy-fifth anniversary of the battle of Gettysburg in Pennsylvania – what better way to get there than by riding their bikes? What better way than to ride the same bike? Elisabeth suggested. Jim thought it a fine way to travel – he was only sorry he'd not thought of it first.

Their tandem bicycle was bought from England. Their friends told them they were crazy and they'd never make it. 'We like being crazy,' they replied and, on 22 April 1939, off they went, dipping their hands ceremoniously in San Francisco Bay before heading eastwards. For the next three months they travelled as 'light vagabonds of the earth', with the name 'Spirit of Fun' painted boldly on their bicycle's frame. That fun had begun straight away, as they learned how to ride the thing: those first wobbly days brought much hilarity. Riding at the back, the stoker would have to place complete trust in the pilot to balance, steer, brake and change gear – this was more than their wedding vows had covered. Everything required coordination and one couldn't pedal without the other; if Jim freewheeled over a bump without warning, Elisabeth would almost fly off her seat. 'Don't lean,' he would tell her; 'Don't spit,' she would retort. They laughed with abandon each time someone shouted, 'She's not pedalling!' as if it were the first time they had heard the joke.

They loved everything about their life on the road: the pace of travel at which they discovered rural America, the crowds and curious looks that their unusual bicycle would draw, and the ravenous appetites that would see them eating 'like hogs, to the amazement of waiters and waitresses wherever we went'.

The Spirit of Fun was a remarkable machine: strong enough to support both of them and all their luggage, the weight-bearing rear wheel remained remarkably low on punctures but high on broken spokes. Taping one spoke to the next until they could find a fix was the solution, until Jim came up with an ingenious idea: removing the spoke by unscrewing it, which he did – but the wrong way. Said Elisabeth, 'With a hiss that Jim deserved, down went the tire.'

Along a network of quiet roads and emerging interstate highways they pedalled – passing truck stops and diners – witnessing the America of the late 1930s recovering in the aftermath of the Great Depression. Most assumed them to be poor, forced to travel by bicycle. Seeking a repair for the broken strap on her camera case, Elisabeth called into a shoemaker, who peered outside to see Jim and the bicycle leaning against the window. When Elisabeth asked, 'How much?' he looked astonished, replying, 'You got money?'

Though quiet, the roads were not always safe, and it was while riding through Wyoming that their journey nearly came to a tragic end: a collision with a truck saw them thrown from the bike, Elisabeth knocked unconscious and Jim badly scraped. It took time for them to recover and for their bicycle to be repaired, and they returned to the road thankful that it hadn't been worse: 'It was good to be on the road again, and it was especially good to be still alive.'

The life of the road was one they loved: the pleasure of riding up to 75 miles per day, the company they would meet and the discovery of how others live. Three months after leaving, they arrived on Virginia Beach and dipped their hands into the waters of the Atlantic – 'Hot dog! We'd done it!' – completing a trans-America bicycle journey that many had ridden before, but none on such a bike as theirs.

They turned around and headed home, finally pedalling into San Francisco five and a half months and 7,000 miles after setting out. It had been the journey of a lifetime, an unforgettable adventure that proved to their friends and family that their dream had been possible. Their emotional return after what might have been the longest tandem trip in the world is familiar to any traveller for whom, no matter how satisfying the adventure or thrilling the experience, there's no place like home. 'Our Bay! Here were the waters of home, and seeing them was a thrill that shook us to our toes.'

Bryan Allen – Flight of the *Gossamer Albatross*

If the wind don't blow, and the chain don't break...

The first week in June is a good time for channel crossings. The settled summer weather has arrived in the northern hemisphere, the hurricane season has not yet begun and hazy dawns followed by light breezes result in calm seas. In 1909, Blériot piloted the first cross-channel flight; 35 years later Eisenhower gave the signal to the D-Day troops to launch. Fast-forward another 35 years, and a team of American aerospace engineers, coastguards and support crew gathered to attempt the first human-powered flight from England to France.

Paul MacCready was the man of the moment. Two years previously his *Gossamer Condor* had won the Kremer International Competition for successfully completing the first figure-of-eight flight in a human-powered aircraft. His new creation, the *Gossamer Albatross*, would be the craft to attempt the 22-mile journey between Folkestone and Cap Gris-Nez. It was a pedal-powered glider, with 48-foot long wings, a long bowsprit protruding from the nose and a large, two-blade propeller driving it forwards. The bicycle part was enclosed in a narrow, deep fuselage, suspended beneath the wings. Bryan Allen would be the man at the pedals.

The team had completed the necessary preparations. They had tested the craft back in the US, had proven its capability to the UK coastguard, and had calculated the time, distance and course necessary for the crossing. The only thing left to do was wait for a suitable weather window.

The first week of June came and went; the wind was just too high. Early the following week, they received the message that conditions were looking better; this might be the best chance they had. They worked through the night, assembling the aircraft, testing parts, checking the control system and preparing for a dawn launch. The air at both coasts was calm, but in mid-channel it was blowing at 5–6 knots. They might not make it even that far. They had little more than a two-hour window before the winds on the far side of the channel would pick up. For the support crew, this was merely a dummy run to test the feasibility of such a project. For Allen and MacCready, this was the only chance they would get. 'The atmosphere was of being on Roosevelt field, Long Island, awaiting the departure of Lindbergh on his flight to Paris.'

At 5.50 a.m., as the sun rose across the water, the *Albatross* made her passage down the makeshift runway and lifted gracefully into the air, heading seawards, a chorus of engines firing up as the support flotilla turned to follow her. For the first 30 minutes, Bryan pedalled the *Albatross*, his well-practised rhythm propelling the craft forwards at a steady 10 knots. The plane glided 15 ft above the swell, 15 or more boats in her wake, a huge white bird heading outwards over the sea.

About half an hour into the voyage, Bryan's radio malfunctioned; though able to receive messages, he was not able to respond. Now that he was isolated from his team, the weight of the mission sat heavily on his shoulders.

A trance-like state soon descended, induced by the steady pedalling, the thrumb of the propellers, and the grey flatness of sea and sky. The odd container ship crossing the bow was all there was to alert Bryan's senses. But approaching the halfway point, the sea began to churn, and waves meant one thing: wind. Bryan pedalled into it, the resistance on the pedals building as he fought to keep the propellers turning at a speed that wouldn't plunge him into the water below. A voice crackled on the radio:

> *If you want to abort the flight and take on a tow, raise an arm to signal.*

Bryan was determined to continue, but his pace had dropped significantly; at this rate he would not reach the other shore in the two and a half hours that had been judged to be the limit of his endurance. There was no land to be seen – the hopelessness of the task seemed to dawn on the support crew just as Bryan seemed to be drawing the same conclusion. After five minutes of persevering into the wind, he gave the signal to receive a tow. As the lead boat *Zodiac* came forward to position herself under the *Albatross*, Bryan flew slightly higher to accommodate her and noticed a sudden improvement; he had moved above the air turbulence and was once more able to pedal unrestricted by headwind. 'Don't hook up yet!' he yelled to the crew below. The mission was back on.

With the two-hour mark passed and 14 miles travelled, the exhaustion of relentless pedalling began to set in. Bryan had carefully calculated his rations for a two-hour flight, conscious of weight, but had now run out of water; his batteries had all but drained, along with those on his altimeter and airspeed indicator. He was flying blind, with no knowledge of how close he was to dropping into the water or falling below stalling speed. Over the radio came, 'Two feet… one foot… six inches… Pedal Bryan, pedal!' Repeatedly, he came perilously close to being swallowed by the sea, and only a superhuman, energy-sapping effort would lift him out of the danger zone.

At 8 a.m. he was still 4.5 miles shy of the shore and on the verge of giving up. Dehydration was becoming a significant problem and his legs were beginning to cramp. The land appeared ahead, but with no shape or substance to give an extra kick of motivation until eventually, a lighthouse emerged through the morning sea mist. Bryan's feeling of relief was short-lived: at least if he had given up in the open channel, his attempt would have been seen as heroic. But here, in sight of land, to surrender was unthinkable! And now, with no water, cramping legs and a coastal breeze threatening to scupper the mission at the last moment, the struggle was at its worst. Bryan dug deep for the final 3 miles, thrusting in turn with legs that were overcome with pain. The inside of his narrow plastic fuselage was hot with the early sun and damp with his breath. He could barely see the beach that would be his landing zone and any error would result in the aircraft being wrecked on the rocks. With 1 mile to go, a red balloon went up on the beach: a transmitter aerial used by French reporters and a perfect homing device to guide Bryan to safety. The *Albatross* hovered over the beach and then alighted, safely, at 8.40 a.m. on 12 June 1979 – 2 hours and 49 minutes after taking off – winning the Kremer Prize of $100,000 for the first human-powered flight from England to France.

Exhausted, elated and with nerves in shreds, the team gathered around Bryan, champagne corks popping in recognition of his heroic efforts. Staggering up the beach came Paul MacCready to shake Bryan by the hand. They exchanged a look; they'd made it by the skin of their teeth. 'Well done kid,' he said. 'Take the rest of the day off.'

Stevie Smith – Pedalling to Hawaii

*What if I were free to do absolutely
anything? What would I do then? What is
the greatest dream I have for myself?*

It's growing dark as the sun sets over the water, the blush of day's end revealing the prickle of thousands of stars. Two friends are sitting in a boat, a pedal-powered boat, the wake gently rippling as they glide into the night. Behind, the coast of Portugal recedes and is swallowed by a haze of sea mist. Ahead is the United States of America, over 4,000 nautical miles away. The pair will spend the next few months making their way across the ocean. 'Mate, I have a confession. I've never spent the night at sea before.' An exchange of glances. 'Me neither.'

It was an outlandish idea that Stevie Smith concocted one day while standing in his office in Paris, looking out at the city skyline and wondering what would become of his life. Desperate to avoid reaching its end having done nothing remarkable, he hit upon the idea of a human-powered circumnavigation of the world. People had cycled, sailed and flown around the world, but no one had done it by human power alone. If he could pedal across the continents, why not pedal across the oceans, too?

Over the next three years his ideas became a reality: years filled with plans, fundraising, setbacks and determination. Finally, Stevie was ready. He had a boat: a purpose-built wooden pedal-powered boat named *Moksha*, Sanskrit for 'freedom'. He had media interest and a film crew, and enough money scraped together to begin. And he had an expedition partner: his friend Jason Lewis. The pair had met at university, a friendship born of taking on eccentric challenges and drinking copious amounts of beer. When Stevie had ventured the idea of the expedition, Jason had agreed without hesitation.

They tested *Moksha* by pedalling her across the channel and then cycled south through France and Spain to Lagos, in Portugal, the port from where they would begin their crossing of the Atlantic Ocean.

Setting their course for Florida, they pedalled into the night. Over the next few months they would see every phase of the cosmos, from the eruption of daybreak to when the sun's dying rays would disappear over the horizon and turn the sky blacker than they had ever imagined. The ocean was impossibly vast, its size and scale difficult to fathom, and they floated in that huge blue expanse with nothing for miles, the horizon blurring where it met the sky. At times the sea mist would thicken and their world would be reduced to a handful of metres on either side. They felt genuine terror when storms would toss *Moksha* like a toy, every sense alert as waves 20 feet high lifted and dropped her while her pilots struggled to keep her upright. They fought headwinds, they fought each other, and they fought the chronic fatigue brought on by sleep deprivation and the long, agonising shifts at the pedals. Nothing ever stayed still. At the mercy of wind and current, there were times when they would be pushed infuriatingly backwards, but finally they reached the trade winds and favourable currents that would pick them up and sling them towards Florida.

Four months in a confined space with one other person was a massive test for both of them. By the time they made landfall the pair had fallen out and agreed to a break: Stevie would cycle a southern course across the United States while Jason would roller skate a central route, then they would reconvene on the west coast for the next ocean crossing.

In San Francisco the expedition nearly stuttered to a halt – lack of funds meant that the next leg looked unlikely. *Moksha* needed repairs, navigational equipment needed replacing and her cabin needed to be stuffed with enough food to last the crossing. They had leaned on friends and family for several years to chase this dream and the debts were mounting. The expedition had become a beast, an impossibly hungry beast. Every waking minute was spent earning money or working out how to earn it. Stevie began to question his motives – the purpose of the whole enterprise had been to break free from the shackles of his past life, but now he was a slave once more, a slave to the expedition. Perhaps it was time to leave it all behind. 'I have proved that I have the courage to do it. Do I also have the courage not to do it?'

Almost a year after arriving in San Francisco, they were ready to take to the water once more. Pedalling beneath the Golden Gate Bridge they set their course for Hawaii, once more engulfed in that watery world where time seemed to stand still and memories of the shore morphed into a life once lived but long forgotten.

Reaching that tiny scattering of islands, a third of the way across the Pacific – four and a half years after leaving and seven years after conceiving of the whole expedition – Stevie came to the conclusion that he had done everything he'd set out to do. He had learned all there was to learn, and he didn't want to do it anymore. It was time for him to put to bed the challenge that he had set himself.

Jason continued alone, pedalling *Moksha* to Indonesia then making his way back to London across Asia and Europe, becoming the first person to circumnavigate the globe by human power alone. Stevie spent some time wandering, trying to find a place to call home, before returning to Salcombe, south Devon, where his mother and sister lived. He was offered a job as the ferryman across the estuary. Strangely enough it was a dream he'd harboured as a child.

Accepting the simplicity of his new work was a struggle at first. For where is the achievement in shuttling a boat back and forth across the same stretch of water all day? But he realised that, if the expedition had taught him anything, goals and accomplishments mean little; their gratification is only temporary. In order to be truly happy, one must enjoy it all, at whatever point, from the beginning to the end. 'Happiness is the acceptance of the journey as it is now, not the promise of the other shore.'

CHAPTER TEN
PUSHING THE LIMIT

Gary Fisher – From klunker to mountain bike

Anyone who rides a bike is a friend of mine.

In the foothills of Carson Ridge in Marin County, California, there is an old fire road that winds through the trees, steep and rough, the compacted dirt dashed with stones, twisting between trunks and boulders, dropping 1,300 feet in less than two miles. In the rain, the mud runs in rivers; when it's dry, the dirt kicks up in great clouds of dust.

This was where Gary Fisher and his mates would hang out, exploring the mountains and drinking beer. The dirt roads were too rough for racing bikes; they would bring their old three-speed newspaper-boy bikes and hurl them down the trails as fast as they dared. It was a hair-raising road – not the most challenging in the place, but with enough twists and turns that riders would have to keep their wits about them to avoid being wrapped around a tree coming off a turn. The bikes would rattle as the hill pulled them down, the rider pumping backwards at the pedals to apply the coaster brake. By the time they reached the bottom, the hub would be burning hot and pouring with smoke, and all the grease would have vaporised. 'Every time you rode the trail you'd have to repack that hub.' The trail became known as Repack.

Gary had always done things differently. A road and track cyclist, he was suspended from racing aged 17 for having long hair. He was one of the first to start modifying his bike to make it better for hurling down a mountain: wide, knobbly balloon tyres, drum brakes from a tandem, motorcycle levers, motorcross handlebars, triple chain rings and extra long cranks. He and his friends named them 'klunkers' and threw them down the hillside as fast as they could.

In October 1976 a race was organised. No one knew what would come of it; Gary's roommate Charlie Kelly, promotor and time-keeper said:

> " *It was just what we did that day,*
> *instead of taking a ride.*

Around ten riders congregated at the top of the Repack, setting off at 30-second intervals. The winner was a man named Alan, who reached the bottom in 5 minutes and 12 seconds, with an average speed of 23 mph. He was the only rider who didn't fall off.

Over the next couple of years Repack races became legendary. It was a backyard sport, practised by a close-knit group; there were no rules or membership requirements other than just to turn up and ride. Word spread and more people joined. Bikes became more heavily modified and speeds increased. Gary set the course record – 4 minutes 22 seconds – which no one has touched, and it's unlikely they ever will.

Gary and Charlie set up the company MountainBikes in 1979 – probably the first time that term was used – and along with other Repack regulars such as Otis Guy and Joe Breeze, popularised and commercialised the mountain bike. The races had petered out by then; with the authorities catching wind of the gatherings, permits were demanded to stage the event. But in its short life, a movement had been sparked, one that paved the way for the modern mountain biking movement.

In 1983, Gary founded NORBA (National Off-Road Bicycle Association), which issued race licences and insurance. Officially licensed, Repack returned for two last hurrahs in 1983 and 1984. Ninety-five competitors rode the final Repack: the first ever sanctioned mountain bike race, and a precursor to what is now a sport recognised and practised by people all over the world.

Danny MacAskill – The Ridge

*I have to be 100 per cent clear I'm going
to do the trick I'm going to do.*

High in the Cuillin mountain range on the Scottish island of Skye stands the Inaccessible Pinnacle. A gargantuan slice of rock, standing 150 ft clear of the mountain, it's a Munro summit topped with a vertical 8 m dorsal fin that stretches into the sky. Far below is the blue sea. Scaling the 'In Pinn' is a challenge to walkers and climbers alike, requiring skill and a head for heights. At the top of the stack stands a man and his bike.

This is Danny MacAskill, a man whose life has been spent obsessed with riding bikes and seeing what tricks he could pull: bunny-hops, backflips, somersaults – Danny can do things on a bike that most people would consider impossible. He's often found riding along the tops of walls, jumping between buildings, pelting up flights of steps and balancing on rails no wider than his tyres. This is high-octane, high stakes and high skill. Danny looks at everything with a mind to riding it – nothing is off-limits.

A professional street trials rider, as a kid he would regularly be brought home by the police for riding on people's walls. Now he encourages children to ride bikes as a way of staying out of trouble. 'Showing schoolchildren what we can do on a bike and getting them into it is the best part of what I do.'

Raised on Skye, Danny had long dreamed of riding along the Cuillin Ridge. The crest runs for 12 km and is one of the best mountaineering routes in Europe, the Holy Grail of scrambling. The Cuillins are remote and pose a serious navigational challenge, as many paths finish in dead ends and sheer drops. Fewer than 10 per cent of the mountaineering parties setting out to conquer the Ridge succeed; of its 12 Munros, the Inaccessible Pinnacle is the most iconic.

The path beneath Danny's wheels drops away as he rolls away from the In Pinn. He's bumping over Collies Ledge – 2.5 feet at its widest, 1 foot at its narrowest – with a 500 ft drop down to Collie Laggan if he were to make a wrong move.

> *I try to picture it like the pavement outside my front garden. Don't go off the kerb. It's all about confidence. You can't think you're going to crash.*

Danny was 23 years old when he shot to fame, a YouTube video of his bicycle stunts making him an overnight internet sensation. He couldn't believe the impact. The renown was enough for him to give up his job as a mechanic so he could ride full time. He has featured in *The New York Times*, has worked as a stuntman and in TV advertisements, and has been nominated as National Geographic Adventurer of the Year. So outlandish are his stunts that some people think they are fake: 'That's the best compliment.'

The path is rutted and stony – patches of mountain-top grass interspersed with tyre-stuttering rocks – and sometimes so narrow it's barely wide enough to accommodate bicycle wheels. It often disappears altogether, leaving just gravel sunk between weathered slabs with a slope falling away on either side. This is route-finding of the highest order, where dead ends mean little – a bunny-hop over an overhanging boulder takes Danny to the next part of rideable track.

His film crew are utterly captivated: 'It's beautiful to watch. Some downhill mountain biking is ridiculous. This is art.'

And they are right. Back down at ground level, Danny rolls smoothly through the meadow, his wheels rumbling with ease, before he casually front-flips over a barbed-wire fence – and is gone.

Nik Wallenda – King of the wire

*I hope what I do inspires people around
the world to reach for the skies.*

Standing on the edge of a building, about to step onto a high wire, Nik Wallenda's heart races. It's not fear that he feels, but respect – respect for the wire, respect for the forces that keep him on the wire and respect for those that might take him plunging to the ground. He steps out. There is no safety net – he puts his trust in his ability and his experience, in his physical and mental strength, and in the training and preparation he has done.

Nik Wallenda comes from a family of aerialists, the 'Flying Wallendas': his mother, father, uncles, grandfather and great-grandfather were all wire-walkers. Nik himself first appeared on a wire even before he was born, as his mother was still performing while six months pregnant. He began wire-walking aged two and then professionally by the age of 13. His parents would teach him to avoid distractions by throwing things at him while he was practising; sometimes they would even fire a gun. Although Nik's heritage was in the circus – his great-grandfather had brought the family to the US from Hungary to perform in the Greatest Show on Earth – he wanted to venture beyond the big top. He began high-wire walking between buildings, taking on more and more extreme challenges. In 2012 he became the first man to walk the wire across the Niagara Falls and, a year later, across a gorge of the Grand Canyon.

In 2008 Nik set out to ride a bicycle on the wire. It was a standard bicycle, with no huge modification apart from having had the tyres and handlebars removed – there would be no need to steer. The bare wheel rims would sit snugly on a wire no thicker than a cigar.

The high wire was rigged between two buildings – it was 72 m long and 41 m above the ground. Nik walked from one end to the other holding his 60-foot long balancing pole. At the platform on the other side he mounted his bicycle and began the return journey.

The ride was quick – quicker than the walk had been. He kept a steady cadence, holding his balancing pole, the bike perfectly upright beneath him. Gradually, steadily, he rode towards the other side.

With a few metres remaining, Nik began to slow down. He had come across an unforeseen problem: the slack of the wire, with the added weight of the bicycle, had resulted in a significant dip. The final few metres would be uphill – not such a problem when walking, but very much so when riding a metal wheel on a metal wire. As the bicycle tilted upwards, the rear wheel lost traction and slipped. The pedals stuttered and the bike wobbled. The spectators gasped. With nerves of steel, Nik caught the movement, rebalanced and resumed the climb. Just a few pedals later, he slowed to a stop. The incline was too great: the bicycle sat static on the line and then started sliding backwards. The tension among the audience was palpable. Nik took a few seconds to gather his composure, balancing for a moment or two absolutely motionless, controlling his breaths. Those seconds seemed to last forever. Nik resumed the slow turn of the pedals that inched the bicycle forwards. This time, the rear wheel kept traction and he rode up and over onto the finish platform. Hands grabbed his balance pole and held onto his bike as he climbed off and went to meet the waiting crowds.

Obviously relieved, he grabbed his kids into a big hug. 'It was a little bit hairy for a minute there…' He took a deep breath. 'I feel great!'

Nik is well aware of the risks of his lifestyle; after all, it's a sport that took his grandfather's life. His challenges grow more unorthodox and more extreme in his quest to chase the next thrill, to do what no man has done before. It's a lifetime of practice that has enabled him to do these things.

> *Don't try this at home! All I want is to inspire people around the world to follow their dreams and never give up.*

Two years later, Nik returned to the wire on his bicycle, this time in the Bahamas – on a line 31 m long and suspended 79 m above the ocean. The day had been filled with high winds, and sporadic lightening flickered on the horizon. But Nik set out above the sea, riding the wire. With a shorter line there was less chance of the uphill climb at the end, and Nik successfully entered the record books for the second time, smashing his own record for the highest bicycle ride in the world.

Rob Jarman – All my own stunts

Throw me off something, I'm pretty much guaranteed to land on my head.

Rob Jarman was really good at falling off his bike. As a child, he would spend hours riding through the woods near his home, finding trails, bouncing between tree trunks, and jumping over roots, across boulders and down rough muddy tracks. Almost every time he rode, he'd have a crash. He'd dust himself off, patch himself up and then try again. He spent more time in the woods than he did at school, chasing more and more difficult sections, riding trails that no one had ever before ridden.

Cycling was an escape. It was a means of going beyond the homestead boundaries and seeing how far he could ride. It was independence. It was a buzz, a thrill, a way to chase those highs where the surge of adrenaline would race through his body and make him feel alive. He was always on the edge, just one misplaced wheel away from tumbling over the handlebars. But there was no fear – the prospect of falling never stopped him. That's what drove him. Cycling taught Rob confidence.

His skills on a bike were such that he started downhill racing, joining the British mountain bike team and going on to race all around the world. What mattered to Rob wasn't chasing the clock, but the beauty of the sport itself: the jumps and tricks, the joy of riding fast down sections where others wouldn't and pushing things to the absolute limit. His riding attracted the eye of photographers and he appeared on the cover of every MTB magazine. They liked his flow and natural style, plus his willingness to try anything.

If there was something extreme to be done on a bike, Rob would do it. He took his mountain bike to Lillehammer, Norway – the venue of the 1994 Winter Olympics – and rode the bobsleigh circuit. He rode a folding bike down a mountain at 70 mph, biked across a slackline and took part in the Yak Attack – a gruelling eight-day race through the Himalayas.

He was never the fastest, but he was the best at crashing. Rob gained notoriety for having the biggest crashes and just walking away. It was a logical progression to train as a professional stuntman.

Being a stuntman on a Hollywood movie and waiting for them to say 'action' was like waiting for the bleep at the World Cup start gate. His background as a mountain biker was really paying dividends. He wanted to jump off all the tallest buildings, crash the fastest cars, and get blown up again and again. He took the fall for Sherlock, trashed thousands of dollars' worth of equipment in the fight scenes for *Prometheus* and was chinned by Bane in *The Dark Knight Rises*.

In 2011, Rob headed out to Italy with the Berghaus team to shoot an advert. He was with a group of extreme adventurers: rock climbers, base jumpers and free runners. They'd had a successful five days of filming and were about to call it a wrap, but decided to have one more go at shooting the biking section; the weather had improved, providing an irresistible setting for one final take.

The film crew set up their kit, ready for action. The shot would show Rob jumping down a near-vertical drop onto a scree-covered slope – it was steep, but not the steepest jump he'd ever taken. They filmed a couple of attempts and then, 'Last shot!' called the director. Rob took the jump – one last time for luck, but his luck was out. The landing was heavy and Rob headbutted the handlebars, cartwheeling down the mountainside. He lay there unmoving as the film crew rushed to his aid. 'I thought he was dead,' the director said. Rob came round as the Mountain Rescue team strapped him to a board and winched him into the air. He had broken his right arm, his collarbone, multiple ribs and his shoulder blade. He had concussion, a bleed on his lung and, more seriously, a bleed on his brain.

Bones, and even lungs, heal over time, but brains are a different story. Six months after the accident, Rob was back to physical health, but it took a further 18 months to sort his head out. 'I am a different person to who I was before I started banging my head for a living.' His accident had a profound impact on his psyche: he would swing between happy and angry, and endure long periods of negativity over his inability to do what he wanted. He needed to get back to who he was: that carefree daredevil who chased that buzz that really made him tick. His bike had nearly cost him his life – but without it he might as well be dead.

Two years after his accident, Rob stood on the slopes of Skiddaw, a 931 m mountain in the Lake District. His aim: to chase the land speed record. Being Rob Jarman, it wasn't going to be an easy route: the mountainside is covered with loose jagged rock, a brutal surface on which to ride. He strapped a flare to the back of his bike and set off, rumbling over the loose scree, juddering and bouncing over rocks as sharp as knives. He reached a top speed of 97 kph, setting the first downhill mountain bike record in the UK. He was gasping as he climbed from his bike at the bottom. 'I thought I would die!' he said. Then he laughed that warm, infectious laugh that seems to trivialise any of the dangers he faces – he was back.

Maria Leijerstam – South Pole cyclist

One of the most important days of my life
was when I learned to ride a bicycle.
MICHAEL PALIN, COMEDIAN AND POLAR EXPLORER

Maria Leijerstam had always wanted to be an adventurer: aged 12, she announced to her mother that she was going to be an astronaut. No stranger to extreme temperatures, in 2007 she had run the Marathon des Sables (desert marathon), 26 miles through arid conditions and 40°C heat, and in 2012 she became the first woman ever to complete the Black Ice Race, traversing the 650 km frozen Lake Baikal in Siberia in seven days, and encountering ferocious storms, cracking ice and sleepless nights in temperatures of below −40°C.

In 2013 she attempted to become the first person to cycle to the South Pole. Others had tried before, but none had succeeded.

Antarctica is vicious: the coldest, driest and windiest continent on the planet – a place twice the size of Australia, with ice as thick as 2 km. Snowsuits regulate core body temperature but extremities can quickly succumb to frostbite. It's the type of place where, if you were to blow your nose, the tissue would instantly freeze. The weather can change rapidly from blinding sunlight to white-out blizzard. Its extreme conditions famously claimed the lives of adventurers Captain Scott and his team. It is a place of seriously challenging terrain, with mountain climbs, glaciers and crevasses forming deep slits way down into the ice.

Two others would be making the attempt at the same time as Maria: American Daniel Burton and Spaniard Juan

Ménendez Granados. It was a race of epic proportions – not only would they be battling with whatever Antarctica threw at them, but they were also competing against each other for the accolade of being the first to cycle to the South Pole. Granados was realistic about the chances of their all making it. 'It's not a race,' said the Spaniard. 'In Antarctica, your chances are 50–50.'

Maria had chosen a shorter route than her two competitors but a more challenging one: following the South Pole Traverse up and over the Transantarctic mountain range. She began her attempt from the edge of the Ross Ice Shelf.

Months had been spent preparing for the trip. Equipment and body were tested to their limits in Siberia, Norway and Iceland; Maria spent a day cycling in an industrial freezer and taught her body to burn fat rather than carbohydrates by training on an empty stomach. Her bicycle was a purpose-built recumbent polar tricycle; rather than perching on a saddle, she would be sitting in a chair, with her legs stretched in front. Three wheels would allow weight to be better spread, the low profile helping her climb and keeping her out of the wind. Aircraft-grade steel was used to ensure it would withstand the extreme temperatures. With 4.5 inch-thick tyres, the bike would bounce across the powdery snow; ski adapters were fitted for when the snow became so deep and soft that the wheels would threaten to sink.

Over a period of ten days, Maria made her way steadily through Antarctica. She battled snowdrifts, high winds and white-outs. She fought the effect that the cold had on her body. Her well-insulated feet sweated inside her snow boots – then the sweat froze. She rode beneath the continuous sun of the Antarctic summer, sleeping for three hours at a time before resuming her journey. Day and night meant little. She endured tough climbs and thrilling descents, making her way around ice shelves and crevasses, across the Leverett Glacier where winds of 100 kph threatened. The terrain sometimes left her with no choice but to drag the bike. The lowest recorded temperature was −29°C, though with wind chill it was effectively much lower.

After 800 km, she reached the geographic South Pole, the first person to have ever done so on a bike. She had beaten her competitors and had claimed the record for the fastest human-powered journey from coast to pole. Despite consuming 4,000 calories per day she had lost 8.2 per cent of her body weight.

Returning with her support team, their snow vehicle making short work of her arduous journey, she passed Juan Ménendez Granados. In a few days he too would reach the pole. 'Congratulations!' he said to Maria as the vehicle slowed to a halt. She hopped out, beaming, and he gave her a heartfelt hug. There's no competition out here – only survival.

Brett Davis – Fat biking Utah's desert canyons

The bicycle is my own form of therapy where I learn what I am truly capable of beyond my own preconceived limitations. It keeps me sane.

The US state of Utah is characterised by expansive plateaus and spectacular canyons: great crevices in the rust-red rock with walls buckled and tilted by centuries of water running steadily towards the sea. These canyons are a Mecca for climbers and a spot for adventure hikers who seek the thrill of exploring some of the most remote, challenging and stunning terrain in the state. The canyon twists and turns as it follows the water course, where rivers lie sunken within sandstone gullies and mud gives way to boulders. A canyon walk might involve climbing, rappelling, scrambling and even swimming. It's not an environment into which one might consider taking a bicycle.

Since first riding a fat bike, Brett Davis has discovered what new heights biking can reach. Fat bikes are the next generation of mountain bikes, with oversized tyres as wide as 4 inches, designed to tackle the powder snow of Alaska and the sandscapes of Mexico. This beast was developed through years of experimentation and became commercially available when Surly launched the Pugsley. The balloon-style tyres, with such extreme width, and pressure as low as 10 psi, seem to float over the terrain. There is no need for suspension.

The fat bike carries the rider to places no other bike could. By riding one, Brett could explore previously untouched sections of trails and, in doing so, push the limits of his mental and physical capabilities. To journey somewhere no one has been before, to pioneer, to reach further than you thought possible would be an antidote to the routine and predictability of the everyday.

Brett and his friend journeyed deep into the canyon region and rappelled down a vertical wall, bikes strapped to backs. 'Once I pull this, there is no going back. We are committed. You good with that?'

'Pull it.' A hundred feet of rope landed at his feet. There was only one way out. Neither knew what the canyon floor would hold, what they would come across between their starting and exit point.

Every pedal was propelling them further into the unknown. They followed the bed of the river, boxed in by steep overhanging walls that stood smoothed by aeons of weather. Swirls of vivid red decorated the stone, which was interspersed with thick vegetation. At times the rock was slick, at times gravel and sand took its place. Their wheels would alternately bounce over boulders and slurp through mud. A shelf of rock might give smooth passage, but bowling ball-sized stones would cause them to stutter. Their concentration was at its highest, the ride engrossing and always changing.

It took a bit of fighting the terrain before Brett settled to the task. 'Relax, let the bike do the work,' he told himself. Each section that presented itself looked as if it might be the one to halt the expedition, but all of them came and went, the oversized tyres making quick work of the mayhem that the canyon bottom presented. The not knowing forced them to embrace the now and live in the moment. There was little else to do – it was as much exhilarating as it was nerve-wracking.

Each time the walls closed in, or impassable boulders lay ahead, dread would pound in their chests. Would this be the end? Scrambling with bikes tested their strength; claustrophobia threatened where low overhangs would require clever wiggling.

Then the river became wider, the banks no longer rideable. Ahead was a murky pool, with no way round, only through. Testing the water with cleated shoes slipping on submerged stone, Brett prepared himself to swim. It was only waist-deep – relief flooded him.

Paw prints told of the creatures that had gone before; a part-buried crank suggested a past adventure.

Eventually, the canyon opened up, the rideable sections becoming longer and easier, and then they were out.

'What began as a potentially foolish idea, to try and navigate a desert canyon by bike, had become a reality. In the process, I redefined what I thought was possible to bike. But more importantly, I ventured out of my comfort zone and recalibrated my tipping point. Sometimes you have to get out of balance to learn what you are capable of.'

Robert Marchand – The centenarian cyclist

I just wanted to do something for my birthday.

On a grey, drizzly, uninspiring day, a group of cyclists make their way to the summit of a col, their weather-beaten peloton tackling the 10 km ascent with eyes fixed on the road in solid concentration. But spirits are high. They reach the top and pop the champagne: one of them, Robert Marchand, is celebrating – he's 103 years old today. And what better way to commemorate such an occasion than to climb the hill that's named after him?

The col Robert Marchand is part of the Ardéchoise, a tough 100+-mile sportive launched in 1992. Marchand took part, aged 81, and has ridden the sportive every year since. In 2011 the col was named after him as a 100th birthday present. He reaches the top with a litheness that belies his years, though it is a bit too cold for him, at a chilly 11°C.

Reaching the age of 100 is an achievement in itself, and to still be cycling is remarkable. Born in France in 1911, Robert Marchand celebrated his 100th birthday by setting the Hour record for his age group, the category having been created especially for him by the UCI. His first outing in a velodrome for 80 years, it came 86 years after his first competitive race, in which he'd falsified his entry on account of not being old enough. At the age of 102 he had another go, breaking his record of 24.25 km to set a distance of 26.93 km.

Another year, another Hour record; his speed increased and at the age of 103 he set his highest distance yet: 26.99 km. Supremely fit – predictably, much more so than most people his age – he has maintained a performance at a greater level than most other sportspeople in the same age bracket. Typically, athletes above the age of 40 experience a decline in fitness of 10–15 per cent per decade. Marchand has declined at around 8 per cent per decade. His Hour record is only 50 per cent slower than Bradley Wiggins's.

He wants to keep racing until he's 105. Then he might stop. 'My doctor tells me I'm doing well and he says to continue what I'm doing – but perhaps to go at it a bit less hard.'

CHAPTER ELEVEN
POSITIVE CHANGE

Kate Rawles – The Carbon Cycle

*I wanted to stride through the land shouting,
'Wake up! This really matters and we
need to do something! WAKE UP!'*

It wasn't so much an epiphany that opened Kate Rawles's eyes to the reality of climate change, but more a gradual realisation that the way we live our lives affects the environment. As a society, we tend not to question what we eat, how we get around, the way we treat our livestock or the manner in which we generate energy. But our over-consumption creates a massive strain on our planet: the demands of our Western lives are so great that we would need three planets to sustain them. As Friends of the Earth say, there is no Planet B.

Kate came to these conclusions while teaching environmental philosophy. Climate change became a buzzword in the late 1990s and she made sure to slip the topic into every lecture. She was amazed, and frustrated, by the apparent lack of public action: why are we not up in arms about what's happening? Are we too comfortable, ill-informed and convinced that if it were that big a problem the Government would do something about it? As a lecturer, it was Kate's job to inform and challenge her students, but not her role to inspire them to actually do anything – the world of academia didn't work that way.

If she couldn't make an impact from a lectern, Kate decided she would do it from the saddle. An outdoor enthusiast, she'd been on several long bike rides before; the bicycle was a wonderful passport to adventure for someone who had never been particularly sporty. The purpose of her ride would be threefold: an expedition to satisfy her wanderlust, a field trip to find out what was happening on the ground in the battle against global warming, and a newsworthy adventure that she could use to raise awareness of climate change, its causes and impact.

Lured by the Rocky Mountains, she headed to the USA. Mountains – her favourite adventure playground, their challenge and beauty unsurpassed by any other landscape – acted as the canary of climate change: any significant alteration in ecosystems would be detected there first. And the USA, as the energy-hungry hub of the Western world, would be the perfect place to explore impacts and attitudes.

She would follow the spine of the Rockies, back and forth across the Great Divide: the geological fault-line that separates the waters that drain to the Pacific and those that drain to the Atlantic. The bicycle was as much a low-carbon method of transportation as a non-threatening one, allowing the perfect platform from which to speak to ordinary people about what climate change means to them and what we should be doing about it. What she'd learned would be taken home to the UK, whose carbon footprint, while lower than that of the USA, was still unsustainably high.

From El Paso on the Mexican border, Kate made her way northwards for 4,000 miles to Alaska. The journey took her through extraordinarily diverse landscapes, from the New Mexican desert to Alaskan glaciers running down to the ocean, with some of the world's most stunning mountain scenery in between. Often hot, often wet — and always, always windy — it was a tough and tiring but fabulous ride. Wildlife and people were the highlights. She encountered bears, wolves, moose, cliff swallows, shimmering aspen and a lynx. Constant generosity and kindness confirmed her belief that 98 per cent of the world is friendly and helpful. 'Heck, honey, are you crazy?' and, 'Can't you afford a car?' was so often followed with, 'Can we buy you lunch?' or, 'Please, take my number in case you ever need help.'

But from the start, her journey revealed some worrying stories: many insisted, 'Climate change? Oh, you don't get that around here!' Then there were the numerous examples of high-energy, oil-hungry, high-consumption lifestyles, the acres of dying forests, the unravelling mountain ecosystems and the steadily retreating glaciers.

Armed with hundreds of pictures, Kate returned home to give presentations under the label 'adventure' — then she talked about climate change as well. Three months on the road had brought home what an extraordinary, diverse, wonderful place Earth is and had left her feeling passionate about the need to protect it. The environmental message was heard by hundreds of audiences, from cycling clubs, book festivals and adventure gatherings, to schools and universities. Her book, *The Carbon Cycle*, was shortlisted for the Banff Mountain Festival Adventure Travel Book Awards. Kate's impact had rocketed beyond her lecture theatre.

Convinced that there really is potential in harnessing the power of adventure to raise awareness and inspire action, in 2016 Kate headed off on another journey – the Life Cycle – to explore the Andes and biodiversity, on a bamboo bike that she built herself. This is 'Adventure Plus': taking to the road with a purpose wider than the voyage itself. Long-distance bicycle touring has always been life-changing for the rider – and Kate had found a way in which it can change the lives of others, too.

Calais Critical Mass

When you move in such numbers, not only does anything feel possible, but your very conception of the possible expands to encompass anything.

It's 10 p.m. on a Friday night. It's dark; rain pummels down. David Charles stands by the side of the road, scalp-plastered hair dripping onto clothes that long ago stopped being waterproof. The remnants of a thunderstorm flicker on the horizon. He's cold, wet and exhausted. Yet David is euphoric. He's one of 80 cyclists who are part-way through their ride from London to Calais. The group have taken 12 hours to ride 45 miles – the journey beset by punctures, steep muddy hills and long detours – but they've just found an 80-seater Chinese restaurant in a Kent village that will give them dinner. There is a yard in which they can leave their bikes. And, in a nearby field, they will have somewhere to sleep.

In dribs and drabs, the cyclists arrive, shattered and ravenous, their misery soon replaced by joy as they hang sodden jackets from plastic chairs and place their orders. The proprietors were preparing for the usual sleepy Friday night with a few locals. They and their restaurant are buzzing.

What are 80 cyclists doing trudging across the countryside in less-than-perfect weather? They are riding their bikes to Calais, to the migrant camp known as the 'Jungle', where they will leave them to be used by the people who live there.

There have always been migrants at Calais, waiting for their chance to cross the English Channel. But wars in Syria and Iraq have caused more people than ever to leave their home countries in search of safety and security. When the French authorities moved the makeshift camp away from the town centre to a new 'tolerated' zone, 7 km away, it left roughly 7,000 people, including women and unaccompanied minors, living in conditions of poor sanitation, with minimal access to support and services.

David was among a group who wanted to do something. He'd visited the Jungle before and met the people who lived there, drunk tea with them and played cricket. He and his friends had the idea that they could ride their bikes to Calais and leave them there, enabling the migrants to more easily access basic essentials like the local shop. They thought they would invite a few others. No one knew how far it would snowball.

The following morning, the 80 cyclists wake, pack tents into bags, rub sleep from eyes and gradually resume their journey to Dover. There, they will crowd the car deck of a ferry, snooze in the lounge or lean against railings while the white cliffs recede and salt-sprayed hair whips about their faces. They will disembark and ride out to the camps where they will find people and shelters and desperation. They will also find hope, kindness and unexpected hospitality when a second night of rain floods their tents and they are invited into the migrants' shelters. It is impossible not to be touched by the tenacity and determination of the occupants of the camps, who must already have overcome so much. David said:

> *Some people came with vague high-minded ideas that they would 'help' the migrants. This... was blown away in that gale. We were their guests.*

And in those words lay the real reason for the ride. Yes, the bicycles would be donated to the migrants, but it wasn't just about 'charity'; it was about the magical force of group optimism: despite the hardships, 80 strangers came together, cycled 65 miles (some having never ridden more than 20) and helped each other. It was about demonstrating the power of cycling: on a bike, anything is possible. But mostly it was about being there, experiencing the reality of which the media reports but a fraction. It was about seeing through the news reports, speaking to people, making connections and having unforgettable experiences. It was about encountering not a 'swarm of migrants' but someone who laughs, cries and gets frustrated – just like you. The migrants had little of material worth, but they had as much to offer as any of us. This was about remembering that they are people, not numbers. By being there, those cyclists felt solidarity with the migrants and took their stories back home.

In many ways, the cycle ride was a ruse. The bikes could have been transported by van. But then only one person would have had that experience. 'One trip to Calais, one cup of hot sugary tea with a Sudanese or Eritrean, is worth a full year of media stories.'

World Naked Bike Ride

Nude not Crude!
Less Gas More Ass!

It's a sight to behold: crowds of cyclists rolling around a city, a massive group occupying the road, and an air of celebration, with bells and whistles and sound systems. The crowd is a rainbow of colours, with fluorescent wigs, flags and banners. But the dominant colour is skin. Bare skin. Most of the cyclists are naked; some wear underwear, while others use body paint to protect their modesty. The message is loud and proud: as bare as you dare. Welcome to the World Naked Bike Ride.

This is a Critical Mass of sorts – a movement through which, by sheer numbers, cyclists reclaim the streets. 'We are not *stopping* traffic, we *are* traffic,' the placards read. It began small, as a protest against oil dependency, but has evolved into a worldwide movement: more than 30 countries hold the annual ride. The messages are many and varied: some ride to celebrate cycling, some to promote positive body image; some ride to highlight climate change, whereas for others it's road danger.

But why naked? This has the shock factor: it makes a noise, a greater impact; it's impossible for the media to ignore. Riding naked is the ultimate freedom; away from the shackles of clothing, it's the epitome of the emancipation that the bicycle has symbolised since its invention. It's a protest against the way in which many people hand over their liberties unknowingly or without thinking. This is a celebration of the human form in its purest sense – not sexualising or idolising – just simple nakedness. It's a protest against the social norm of clothing. Why should the naked human body be so shocking? Is it because of the sexualisation of our society? It's reminiscent of the scandal that Tessie Reynolds caused, wearing pantaloons that revealed her ankles and calves. Perhaps the Victorian pioneers of 'rational' dress rode their bicycles naked when away from the prying eyes of men; the swimmers of that age certainly did, their cumbersome body suits hazardous. It's a protest against the indecent exposure of people to cars and the pollution they create. And for those who are tired of hearing the commonly used phrase, 'Sorry, mate, I didn't see you,' their message is loud and clear: you can see me now.

CK Flash and Peckham BMX

If I never got involved in BMX I'd
probably be in prison right now.
MEMBER OF PECKHAM BMX

On a patch of waste ground between two estates controlled by rival gangs is a rudimentary BMX track. There is space for only a handful of jumps; the surface is rough and unpaved. Broken bottles lie discarded at the edges from night-time over-consumption; a training session begins by sweeping the glass away. A few kids ride the track, their talent obvious. They spend hours practising while all around groups of youths sit in tower block stairwells. This is Peckham, London, a place which frequently finds itself in the news for the wrong reasons: shootings, drug deals, knife crime and murdered teenagers. It was an epicentre of the 2011 riots, where gangs rampaged through the streets, looting, smashing shop fronts and starting fires. It was where Damilola Taylor lost his life, at ten years old, in one of the most high-profile killings in the country.

CK Flash, a DJ and entrepreneur, grew up in Peckham. He had friends in gangs; his after-school time could have been spent getting in trouble. But CK had a talent: BMX. While his mates were hanging around, he would be out riding his bike, training for the next competition. His bike was his ticket to escape, his way off the streets; he knew how valuable having such a focus could be for kids who had little other direction. When Southwark Council approached him to ask if he could build a BMX track in Peckham, he instantly said yes.

The space available was tiny; there would be room for a mere quarter-size track. People ridiculed him. 'Peckham having a BMX club is like Jamaica having a bob-sled team,' they said. But CK didn't listen, and after much perseverance and hard graft, the track was built. With a membership of four, Peckham BMX opened.

It was a tough fight, trying to sell BMX in a rough area of London where some kids can't even afford a bike. But CK knew the benefit this club could bring to the community and worked hard to make a success of it. Every time he asked for something, the answer would be 'no', but he never gave up and kept searching until he found another way through.

> *I am where I am today because I won't take no for an answer. There's always a way round – you just have to keep looking until you find it.*

In the following months, membership boomed. Two of the members, Tre Whyte and Quillon Isador, showed promise. 'We're gonna take them to the worlds,' CK said. But two kids from Peckham, training on a quarter-size track with no surface, are hardly World Championship contenders. He asked for a bigger track but, again, the answer was no. He had something to prove. 'If they can win on a tiny track with no surface, just think how good they will be when they get to a proper track.'

It wasn't just the lack of training facilities that stood in their way. While Quillon was lucky to have the support of his family, Tre had moved out of his home as a teenager. Both felt the pressure of gang culture within their neighbourhood, negative stereotypes of 'young black men in hoods' and competition from others with sponsorship and proper tracks. But their talent shone through, nurtured by CK, who pushed them with his unshakable commitment. Within five years of the track opening, Tre had won the nationals and qualified for the Olympics, and they had both been accepted onto the

British Cycling BMX team. In 2012 Quillon became the under-16 world champion.

Peckham BMX finally got its full-size track. There are now around 180 members. 'We have a mix of good kids and those that need help in life,' CK says. 'It's good for them. It keeps them out of trouble. It teaches them discipline, to be on time, to eat right, to look after themselves. It's an activity that anyone can do, and that everyone enjoys.' Some of the more troubled kids in the club have come from Pupil Referral Units. Riding with Peckham BMX means that some of them are back in mainstream schools. 'We help the kids to be the best they can be.'

World Bicycle Relief – Power of bicycles

Affordable, reliable mobility is no doubt one of the most valuable but unrecognised tools of relief and development work.

In 2004, a tsunami crashed through the Indonesian subcontinent, destroying homes and devastating communities. Upwards of 200,000 people lost their lives. Watching from his home in Chicago, Illinois, F. K. Day felt moved to do something. Vice-president of SRAM, the bicycle components company, he was aware of the power of the bicycle.

With an idea of what mobility might mean to tsunami victims and relief workers, it felt strangely within my reach to help.

An inexpensive, sustainable form of mobility, a bicycle can make the difference between seeing a doctor, getting to school and making a living, or not. Day contacted aid organisations with his idea: could he send bicycles? No, just send money, was the response. So convinced was he that bicycles could help that he jumped on a plane to speak to the organisations face to face. The reaction was wholly different; hesitant but hopeful, they asked, 'You can do this?' Within a year he had arranged the building of 24,000 bicycles for Sri Lankan families: 'Buffalo Bicycles' that were locally made and rugged enough to cope with the environment in which they were to be used. This was the start of World Bicycle Relief.

Very quickly the power of the bike to improve lives became apparent. A bicycle can travel four times the distance and offers five times the carrying capacity of foot travel. One man, a fisherman who had lost his boat and supplies in the tsunami, was able to use the bike to sell vegetables and fish door-to-door, while bringing his daughter to school on the way. For others, having a bicycle meant they had extra time, money and energy to devote to rebuilding their lives. This simple machine had moved beyond merely providing relief – it had become integral to people's livelihoods.

In 2006, F. K. Day was contacted by a group that worked in Africa, where inhabitants were victims of extreme poverty and disease. Work began in sub-Saharan countries, including Zambia, Kenya and Zimbabwe. Buffalo Bicycles were manufactured to be given to volunteer HIV/AIDS care givers, enabling them to access remote villages, so they could visit and help more people on their rounds, as well as administering medication more quickly. Schoolchildren, many of them rising before dawn to walk up to 10 miles a day to get to a school, were given bicycles; they no longer arrive at school exhausted, hungry and late. Freedom of transport can be a major route out of poverty. For girls particularly, many of whom suffer harassment on the long walk, a bicycle can mean safety. Of the 60,000 bicycles provided, 70 per cent went to girls.

Key to the project's success is sustainability: for every 50 bikes provided, one mechanic is trained. Bicycles are purpose-built in the local area, making them appropriate for the terrain and local environment, and ensuring that replacement parts are readily available.

World Bicycle Relief has now provided its 200,000th bicycle. For the schoolchild, healthcare worker or entrepreneur who can travel further, save time and carry heavy loads, each one represents a life-changing new beginning.

Sunny Chuah – Bamboo biking the Silk Road

Think of bicycles as rideable art that can just about save the world.
GRANT PETERSEN

Sunny Chuah from Singapore first had the idea of using bamboo as a building material when he saw his grandmother use a bamboo pole to hang his wet and heavy army uniform. Its strength amazed him. Five times stronger than steel, durable and shock absorbent, lightweight, versatile, and growing in tubular form, it seemed an obvious material from which to build a bike. It would be the ultimate ecofriendly mode of transport: a bicycle made from a fast-growing natural material that, during its lifetime, produces 35 per cent more oxygen than other trees. Bamboo bicycles had been made as early as 1894, but though well-received, they did not become widely popular. Sunny tested a few prototypes and finally built a bicycle of which he was proud. He decided to demonstrate its worth by riding it 6,000 km along the Silk Road.

The longest trade route in the world, stretching one-third of the way around the equator from Europe to China, its rough surface has been trodden by centuries of camels, mules, carts and human feet. Sunny crossed the Pamir highway in Central Asia, wandering through snow-covered passes 4,200 m above sea level. Heading west, he chased the sun through the scorching deserts of China, the road connecting oases that would once have been a hubbub of trade and a place of rest for travellers. His bike carried him up and down mountains, across Gobi sand and through tyre-sucking gravel. There were moments when riding was impossible, and he would have to push. But his bike was light, despite the luggage, and the frame absorbed the vibrations of the road. He arrived in western China brimming with affection for his steed.

The expedition was called the 'Circle of Life'; using natural materials and relying on the kindness of strangers, he trekked across this inhospitable land. The purpose of the ride was threefold: merging his love of bikes and adventure, indulging his passion for entrepreneurship, and putting into action the cause of eco-tourism which was close to his heart. He was also searching for answers: by reliving the magic of the ancient Silk Road, could he look ahead to the future of tourism, making adventure and travel more sustainable?

After returning home to Singapore, he finished his degree in Business Management and began to put into action the many plans he'd formed while riding the Silk Road. He now runs a company, Bamboobee, which produces and sells bicycles, kids' balance bikes and DIY bicycle kits. His dream of a bamboo bicycle revolution is becoming a reality, as around the world, dozens of companies now make bikes from this material. As each bamboo cane is different, every bike is unique. According to his customers, riding one is like riding on air. It's just another way in which the bicycle can save the world.

The Dallaglio Flintoff Cycle Slam

When I see an adult on a bicycle, I do not despair for the future of the human race.
H. G. WELLS

Every year, thousands of people raise money for charity by riding their bikes. It's something that appeals to seasoned riders, as well as those who rarely, if ever, take to the saddle. Charities capitalise on this enthusiasm for mass bike ride challenges – with each one, more people are discovering the joy of riding as well as raising potentially huge amounts for their chosen cause. It leads to the almost inevitable question that people ask when someone undertakes a ride of any kind: 'Is it for charity?'

From April to May 2012, rugby legend Lawrence Dallaglio and cricket superstar Andrew 'Freddie' Flintoff teamed up for the Dallaglio Flintoff Cycle Slam, a 2,872-mile ride from

Olympia, Greece – the ancient birthplace of the Olympics – to Stratford, London, the location of the 2012 Games. For three and a half weeks they rode, from the glittering coastline of the Italian Riviera and the white gravel streets of the Tuscan *strade bianche*, to the precipitous Swiss Alps and the infamous 'Hell of the North' cobbled section of the Paris–Roubaix cycle race. The final leg was 100 km from Ashford in Kent to the Olympic stadium in east London. Along the way they were joined by celebrity friends and members of the public – a team numbering 250 spread across the five stages of the ride.

It was tough: they rode up to 180 km per day, the climbs proved to be more difficult than they thought and the weather was unpredictable. They battled heat, headwinds and hail, exhaustion, hunger and the inevitable saddle sores, pulling through as a team with an incredible sense of camaraderie that cajoled and carried everyone to the finish line.

Neither Flintoff nor Dallaglio are natural cyclists; not particularly built for hours in the saddle, they both required custom-built Boardman frames. Emotions and tears were abundant, especially when, after 22 days of riding, they reached the Olympic Stadium and could finally stop. Their aim had been to raise a sum to represent the year of the Games: £2.012 million for Cancer Research and Great Ormond Street Hospital. They smashed the target.

Flintoff remarked:

> *It was more rewarding than probably anything I've achieved in sport – which is just hitting a ball and trying to catch one or throw one*

– whereas this is affecting lives and it's making a big difference.

And in Dallaglio's words:

> *When you are in a group and you do it together it's a very special feeling. One of the reasons that I love bike rides is that, apart from having fun, everyone works together with a purpose, pursuing the same target and feeling the same sense of achievement.*

Otesha – Wheels of change

Otesha changed my life.
ANNA HUGHES

In the summer of 2012 I spent six weeks pedalling around the South West of England with a group of eight women. We rode from the luscious Wye Valley on the border of England and Wales, through the plains of Gloucestershire and Somerset to the vicious hills of Dartmoor.

Our trip had everything one might expect from a bicycling tour: impressive mileages, challenging terrains and weather that ranged from throat-parching heat to luggage-saturating downpours. Along towpaths, country lanes and disused railway lines we rode, lugging trailers piled high with equipment up near-vertical inclines. We slept on hillsides in farmers' fields and watched shooting stars fill the sky.

We camped in barns and in forest clearings, and pitched our tents by the gently lapping waters of the Dart in the shadow of vineyards. Cycling from remote countryside to bustling cities, clothes grime-encrusted from long days in the saddle, we begged our way into sports centres to wash our hair. Everything was accompanied by the subtle smell of woodsmoke. Our food was a luxurious collection of vegetables provided by local farms, cooked each night on our camping stove.

But this was no ordinary tour. Eight strangers, we had been drawn together by the Otesha Project, a social enterprise with sustainability at its core. United by an enthusiasm for cycling and the environment, we pedalled around the country, spreading an environmental message. All of us were volunteers, some experienced cyclists, some not so, all young and passionate and hoping to create change.

Otesha is a Swahili word meaning 'cause to dream'. The project was founded by two Canadians, Jessica Lax and Jocelyn Land-Murphy, who met in a travelling field school in Kenya in 2002 and experienced first-hand the effects of climate change on the African nation. The global repercussions of our Western consumer lifestyles suddenly seemed very real. In that moment they resolved to live more sustainably, impacting as little upon the environment as possible.

As they made small adjustments to their daily habits, the power of the individual to make a difference became apparent; personal change is often the only thing within our means, and it can be a powerful tool. And if they could make changes, why couldn't others? What revolution could they spark if this mindset were to spread amongst Canada's youth? Jessica and Jocelyn suddenly had cause to dream.

A year later they set off on a 164-day bicycling adventure from one side of Canada to the other, with 33 members in their team, giving presentations to more than 12,000 young people across the country. Through a mixture of drama and workshops, they examined how lifestyle choices can affect our environment, inspiring audiences of young and old alike.

> *It's about re-evaluating our daily choices to reflect the kind of future we'd like to see – rethinking what we really need, conserving resources, and voting with our consumer, citizen and community power.*

That was the very first Otesha Project Cycle Tour. The organisation spread across the world, with projects springing up in Australia, the Philippines, France and the UK. Each year, groups of cyclists take to the road to spread the message of environmental sustainability and social justice. This is how I found myself riding with these women.

In every location we visited, our play and workshops were presented to schools, youth clubs and community groups. The purpose was to inspire people to question the choices we make each day: what we eat, wear or buy, as well as how we clean ourselves, use energy and travel around. As we journeyed further into the tour, it became clear that it wasn't just the audiences that would be influenced: it was us. Cycling from place to place, we discovered the joyous simplicity of living on the road. Our vegan diet was more than sufficient to keep us energised and happy over those long hours spent in the saddle. We sought out local community projects and shops rather than following the mainstream. The workshops that we ran with the children opened our eyes to issues we tended not to question.

I have been vegan ever since. No longer do I shop in supermarkets; it's very rarely that I buy clothes from anywhere other than a charity shop. I consider air miles; I always buy organic. I try to resist the pull of advertising. Living without a shower for six weeks forced me to wash my hair less frequently, a habit which stuck; the old adage that the more you wash the more you need to wash, and hair will start to clean itself if you leave it long enough, is true. I use less and I waste less. I step a little lighter on the world. I am not a different person but I do things differently.

There were hundreds of other things that I could have done that summer – necessary, important, mundane things – but they would have faded into the blur of the past after a while. Yet I will remember that trip for the rest of my life. Early on we were asked to share with the group our motivation for having signed up; I said that I wanted everyone to fall in love with cycling. That's what motivates me: the simple joy of riding – the fresh air and the freedom that people have felt ever since this remarkable machine was invented. I would far rather spend a few months on a bicycle than a few hours on a plane. It's about making the journey mean as much as the destination. It's amazing how much one can achieve on a bicycle: we travelled substantial distances with relative ease, and though our equipment was heavy and extensive, we hauled it all with us. It's the simple fact that each epic journey begins with a single pedal stroke. As a form of exercise, it can make an athlete of the most unlikely of riders. Yes, it's frustrating when the winds always seem to be headwinds, tyres puncture and the trailer breaks as you are crawling up a long incline. But the empowerment, the freewheeling, the fresh air, the freedom, the sun, the sky, the views, the strength, the camaraderie and the cake-scoffing make it all worthwhile.

Otesha eventually closed its operations in the UK and Canada, 13 years after that grassroots idea sparked a worldwide project. But those years were packed with bicycle tours and workshops and theatre presentations and youth engagement activities. In that time it reached hundreds of thousands of young people and gave them an alternative to the lifestyle choices with which we tend to be presented. There's no way to measure the true impact of the work of Otesha. But as well as meaning 'cause to dream', Otesha also means 'cause to grow'. The seed of change has been planted. Maybe now it will grow.

BIBLIOGRAPHY AND FURTHER READING

Buhring, Juliana *This Road I Ride: My Incredible Journey from Novice to Fastest Woman to Cycle the Globe* (2016, Piatkus)

Crane, Richard and Nicholas *Journey to the Centre of the Earth* (1987, Bantam)

Earley, Breifne *Pedal the Planet: One Man's Journey from the Depths of Despair to Winning the World Cycle Race* (2016, BE Press)

Hughes, Anna *Eat, Sleep, Cycle: a Bike Ride Around the Coast of Britain* (2015, Summersdale)

Little, Nan *If I Can Climb Mt. Kilimanjaro, Why Can't I Brush My Teeth? Courage, Tenacity and Love Meet Parkinson's Disease* (2015, CreateSpace Independent Publishing Platform)

Mercer, Danae *A Long Ride Home: How Riding from Beijing to London Fixed a Broken Cyclist* (2014, The Guardian)

Murphy, Dervla *Full Tilt: Ireland to India with a Bicycle* (2010, Eland Publishing Ltd)

Mustoe, Anne *A Bike Ride: 12,000 miles around the world* (1992, Virgin Books)

Penn, Robert *It's All About the Bike: The Pursuit of Happiness On Two Wheels* (2011, Penguin)

Rawles, Kate *The Carbon Cycle: Crossing the Great Divide* (2012, Two Ravens Press)

Reid, Carlton *Roads Were Not Built for Cars: How Cyclists Were the First to Push for Good Roads & Became the Pioneers of Motoring* (2015, Island Press)

Smith, Stevie *Pedalling To Hawaii: A Human-Powered Adventure* (2004, Summersdale)

Stoll, Scott *Falling Uphill* (2010, Argonauts)

Van den Berg, Eric *Home is Elsewhere: Heinz Stücke: 50 Years Around the World by Bike* (2015, Brompton Bicycle Ltd)

Willgress, Graeme *Riding2Recovery: a Journey within a Journey* (2012, blurb.com)

Zheutlin, Peter *Around the World on Two Wheels: Annie Londonderry's Extraordinary Ride* (2008, Citadel Press Inc.)

Have you enjoyed this book?
If so, why not write a review on your favourite website?

If you're interested in finding out more about our books,
find us on Facebook at **Summersdale Publishers** and
follow us on Twitter at **@Summersdale**.

Thanks very much for buying this Summersdale book.

www.summersdale.com